RENAISSANCE

VOLUME 1

Africa — Bologna

GROLIER
EDUCATIONAL

Published by Grolier Educational
Sherman Turnpike
Danbury, Connecticut 06816

© 2002 Brown Partworks Limited

Set ISBN 0-7172-5673-1
Volume 1 ISBN 0-7172-5663-4

Library of Congress Cataloging-in-Publication Data

Renaissance.
    p. cm.
Summary: Chronicles the cultural and artistic flowering
known as the Renaissance that flourished in Europe and
in other parts of the world from approximately 1375 to
1575 A.D.
Includes index.
Contents: v. 1. Africa–Bologna — v. 2. Books and libraries–
Constantinople — v. 3. Copernicus–Exploration — v. 4.
Eyck–Government — v. 5. Guilds and crafts–Landscape
painting — v. 6. Language–Merchants — v. 7. Michelangelo–
Palaces and villas — v. 8. Palestrina–Reformation — v. 9.
Religious dissent–Tapestry — v. 10. Technology–Zwingli.
    ISBN 0-7172-5673-1 (set : alk. paper)
    1. Renaissance—Juvenile literature. [1. Renaissance.]
I. Grolier Educational (Firm)
    CB361 .R367 2002
    940.2'1—dc21
                        2002002477

For information address the publisher:
Grolier Educational, Sherman Turnpike,
Danbury, Connecticut 06816

FOR BROWN PARTWORKS

Project Editor: Shona Grimbly
Deputy Editor: Rachel Bean
Text Editor: Chris King
Designer: Sarah Williams
Picture Research: Veneta Bullen
Maps: Colin Woodman
Design Manager: Lynne Ross
Production: Matt Weyland
Managing Editor: Tim Cooke
Consultant: Stephen A. McKnight
                            University of Florida

Printed and bound in Singapore

ABOUT THIS BOOK

This is one of a set of 10 books that tells the story of the Renaissance—a time of discovery and change in the world. It was during this period—roughly from 1375 to 1575—that adventurous mariners from Europe sailed the vast oceans in tiny ships and found the Americas and new sea routes to the Spice Islands of the East. The influx of gold and silver from the New World and the increase in trade made many merchants and traders in Europe extremely rich. They spent some of their wealth on luxury goods like paintings and gold and silver items for their homes, and this created a new demand for the work of artists of all kinds. Europe experienced a cultural flowering as great artists like Leonardo da Vinci, Michelangelo, and Raphael produced masterpieces that have never been surpassed.

At the same time, scholars were rediscovering the works of the ancient Greek and Roman writers, and this led to a new way of looking at the world based on observation and the importance of the individual. This humanism, together with other new ideas, spread more rapidly than ever before thanks to the development of printing with movable type.

There was upheaval in the church too. Thinkers such as Erasmus and Luther began to question the teachings of the established church, and this eventually led to a breakaway from the Catholic church and the setting up of Protestant churches—an event called the Reformation.

The set focuses on Europe, but it also looks at how societies in other parts of the world such as Africa, China, India, and the Americas were developing, and the ways in which the Islamic and Christian worlds interacted.

The entries in this set are arranged alphabetically and are illustrated with paintings, photographs, drawings, and maps, many from the Renaissance period. Each entry ends with a list of cross-references to other entries in the set, and at the end of each book there is a timeline to help you relate events to one another in time.

There is also a useful "Further Reading" list that includes websites, a glossary of special terms, and an index covering the whole set.

Contents

VOLUME 1

Africa

At the time the Renaissance was happening in Europe, Africa was also going through an important period of its history. During this time some of the most powerful and influential of all African civilizations arose. They became important centers of learning and culture, and grew wealthy through trade and conquest. In the 14th and 15th centuries African scholars such as the historian Ibn Khaldun did much to further people's understanding of the world. At the same time, tales of the riches of African kings such as Mansa Musa spread throughout both the Muslim Middle East and Christian Europe.

At the beginning of the 14th century several powerful empires and dynasties existed in Africa, both north and south of the Sahara Desert. Many African states had thriving economies. The continent was crisscrossed by a network of trading routes that not only joined the various regions to one another, but also linked Africa to the wider world. Routes across the Sahara kept Europe and the Arab world supplied with gold, ivory, and slaves and helped satisfy the African demand for salt and metalware.

NORTH OF THE SAHARA

By the 14th century Europe and North Africa had already had close links for hundreds of years. Since the early eighth century Muslims from northern Africa had controlled parts of Spain. The Europeans knew these people as Moors. From 1336 to 1358 the Arab

Marinid dynasty of Morocco controlled most of North Africa as well as Granada in southeastern Spain. After 1358 the Marinids lost power to the Ziyanid and Hafsid dynasties in lands to the east of Morocco.

Arabic kingdoms survived in Spain until 1492, when the last Moorish king was driven out by an alliance of Spanish Christian kingdoms. Between 1497 and 1535 the Spanish captured the North African cities of Melilla, Oran, Algiers, Bougie, and Tunis. Spanish influence in North Africa did not last long, however. In 1517 the Ottomans from the region that is now Turkey took Egypt from the Mamluks. During the course of the 16th century

Above: This ornamental mask carved from ivory dates back to the 16th century and was made by the Edo people from the region that is now Nigeria. The top of the mask is decorated with a row of tiny heads, intended to represent Portuguese traders.

Right: This map of Africa shows the areas covered by the major African states at the beginning of the 16th century, as well as some of the most important cities at that time.

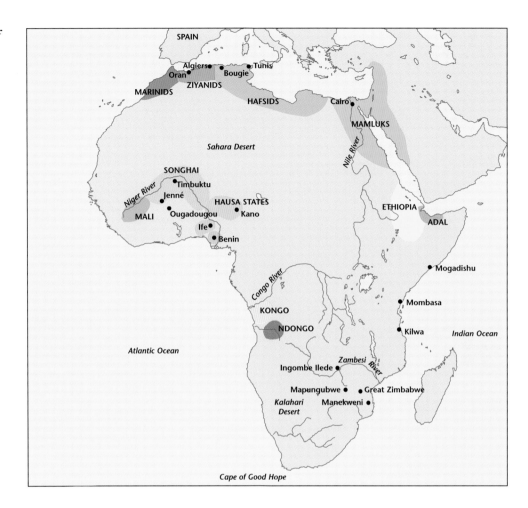

Ottoman control spread westward across northern Africa, forcing out the Spanish garrisons. By 1570 the Islamic empire of the Ottomans covered all of the continent's Mediterranean coast apart from Morocco.

THE SUDAN

One area that was home to many important states was the Sudan region, which was made up of the semideserts and dry grasslands that lay to the south of the Sahara Desert. One of the most successful of these kingdoms was Mali. It reached its height in the mid-14th century, when it covered present-day Gambia, Senegal, Guinea-Bissau, parts of Mauritania, much of modern Mali, and even southern Algeria. The rulers of Mali controlled both the trade from the goldfields of present-day Ghana and the trade routes that led north across the Sahara Desert to the Mediterranean and Europe.

The most famous king of Mali was Mansa Musa (reigned about 1312–1337). In 1324 he made a famous pilgrimage to Mecca that turned into such an extravagant display of wealth that Arab chroniclers wrote about the event for years. Each of his 500 servants carried a golden staff, while a caravan of 100 elephants carried 10,000 lb. (4,500kg) of gold between them. In the course of his journey Musa stopped over in Cairo and spent so much money there that he devalued the Egyptian currency. During his reign the Sankore mosque in Timbuktu became a center of Islamic learning, and the foundations for the University of Sankore were laid.

THE PORTUGUESE IN AFRICA

Until the early 15th century very few Europeans had set foot on the continent of Africa, and much of its vast interior had never been seen by European eyes. Many people had, however, heard tales of the incredible riches of African kings such as Mansa Musa. They had also heard stories of lost kingdoms, such as that of the legendary Christian king Prester John, and tales of the strange and wonderful animals that explorers had brought back from the region. To the Europeans of the Renaissance, therefore, the continent of Africa seemed an exotic, exciting world that offered limitless possibilities.

The main reasons behind the wave of exploration that occurred in the 15th century were commercial, however. Under the instructions of Prince Henry the Navigator (1394–1460) a number of Portuguese explorers sailed down the west coast of Africa, setting up trading depots on the way. These enabled them to profit from the extremely lucrative African trade in gold and slaves. The Portuguese were also trying to find a sea route to India. They eventually did so in 1488 when the explorer Bartholomeu Dias (about 1450–1500) sailed around the Cape of Good Hope, the southernmost tip of Africa.

The empire of Mali dominated west Africa until the middle of the 15th century, when it began to be over-shadowed by the growing state of Songhai that lay to the east. During the reigns of Sonni Ali (ruled 1464–1492) and Askia Muhammad I (ruled 1492–1528) Songhai developed into a vast and well-administered empire. Both Mali and Songhai had walled cities with spectacular mosques, including the famous one at Jenné. Despite its military might, Songhai was conquered by Morocco in 1591.

THE ATLANTIC COAST

In the forests and more heavily wooded grasslands south of the Sudan region many states existed long before the arrival of Europeans along the Atlantic coast in the late 15th and early 16th centuries. Most were based around internal trade routes that ultimately led north to the Sahara Desert. Legends say that 15th-century horsemen from northern Ghana founded the first Mossi kingdoms, such

Below: The mosque at Jenné in Mali, which was built originally in the 14th century. Made out of mud bricks, the mosque has been continually rebuilt over the centuries, although its layout has not changed.

as Dagomba and Wagadugu (present-day Ougadougou). In the north of what is now Nigeria, independent Hausa city-states such as Kano, Katsina, Kebbi, and Zaria had existed for hundreds of years. These walled towns each had their own royal family.

Farther south the Yoruba people had also been living in towns for centuries, all claiming descent from the founders of Ife, one of several Yoruba kingdoms. The 14th century was a time of great prosperity for Ife, which was then dominant over Benin in the southeast. Many of the bronze heads and figures for which Ife is famed were produced during this period.

THE EAST COAST

Along the coast of eastern Africa centuries of trade with Arabs, Persians, Indians, and other Africans had allowed Swahili city-states such as Kilwa, Mogadishu, and Mombasa to prosper by the early 13th century. Goods from inland, as well as local exports such as silk and timber, were traded for luxury goods from Asia and Arabia. The Swahili merchants lived in fine houses made from stone and coral. Their towns were encircled by stone walls and ruled by sheikhs or sultans.

To the northwest of these Swahili city-states lay the Christian kingdom of Ethiopia, the most recent of many that had long dominated the highlands. The people were ruled by kings who claimed descent from the biblical King Solomon. The rich often worshiped in churches carved out of rock below ground level, the most famous of which were at Lalibela.

Ethiopia often came under threat from its Islamic neighbors, in particular in 1526, when the ruler of the Muslim kingdom of Adal started a holy war against it. However, with the military help of Portugal the Ethiopian emperor Lebna Dengel managed to defeat his Islamic enemies and keep his kingdom Christian.

CENTRAL AFRICA

In the heart of Central Africa, far from any coastal ports, powerful regional trading centers existed. Centers such as Ingombe Ilede, Manekweni, and Mapungubwe all benefited from long-distance trade, mostly in gold but also in copper.

From the 14th to the mid-15th centuries, however, these places were overshadowed by Great Zimbabwe. This famous walled city, once home to 18,000 people, was the most impressive of the Shona people's many zimbabwes, meaning "stone houses." The city was the center of a vast empire, which at one stage stretched from the Kalahari Desert in the west to the Indian Ocean in the east. However, in the late 15th century the empire's rulers shifted their power base north. Soon afterward the empire splintered into many smaller kingdoms.

Above: The ruins of the central enclosure at Great Zimbabwe. The walled town was the center of a huge empire that spread over much of southern Africa in the 15th century.

SEE ALSO
♦ Exploration
♦ Islam
♦ Ottoman Empire
♦ Portugal
♦ Spain

Agriculture

Left: An illustration from a 15th-century French manuscript showing peasants building a fence on their lord's land. In the distance other peasants can be seen plowing and scattering seed.

In the 14th century most of the people living in Europe were peasant farmers. They worked from dawn to dusk, laboring in the fields to grow the grain that would be made into bread, which was the main food for everyone at that time. Farming had remained the same for centuries, but the next 200 years were to see profound changes. Farmers started to grow many different crops and to sell them in far-distant markets. Raising livestock for meat and wool was also to become important.

During the Middle Ages farming was based on large estates called manors. The peasants who lived on a manor produced food for the lord of the manor and his dependents, military retainers, and household servants, and fodder for the animals he kept for work, war, and sport. Most peasants were serfs. This meant that they were virtually slaves and were not allowed to leave the manor. On the other hand, the land where they lived and worked could not be taken from them. While peasants who were serfs may have been bound to the soil, it was also true that the soil was bound to the peasants.

Nevertheless, the life of a peasant was hard, and he and his family could scarcely scrape a living. They had to give much of what they grew to the lord of the manor and were only allowed to keep barely enough for their own needs. They also had to spend time working for the lord and had to pay to use his facilities for such tasks as milling grain and baking bread.

SYSTEM BREAKING DOWN

By the beginning of the 14th century this system was beginning to break down in western Europe. Some landlords started to lease part of their manor to tenant farmers. Others allowed peasants to pay rent for their land instead of giving labor service. Then the Black Death (the plague) swept across Europe, killing about one-third of the population. This meant that a large part of the rural workforce was wiped out, and landlords found it difficult to find people to work their farms. The demand for labor led to greater economic freedom, and many serfs were able to become free tenants.

Above: Peasants threshing grain in a barn at harvest time. Threshing involved beating the cereal harvest with sticks to separate the grain from the stalks.

The Black Death also meant there was plenty of food for the people who survived, and this brought the price of grain down. A new industry emerged, beer-brewing. It was based on cheap grains and the discovery that a vine called hops acted as a preservative—so the beer could be transported to distant markets for the first time.

In other places cereal production gave way to wine. In regions known to be favorable for wine-growing, new vineyards were planted. Other crops also started to be grown for market. Rice, peas, asparagus, spinach, melons, and oranges all became profitable crops in areas suitable for their cultivation.

ANIMALS ON PASTURES

Following the plagues of the 14th century, some farmland was left uncultivated and turned back into forest and wetlands. Other uncultivated lands grew grasses rich in minerals, which made them excellent pasture land. So farmers started to keep animals on these lands instead of trying to grow crops.

Animals were kept not only for meat, but also for their hides and, in

SUGAR

Sugar was extremely expensive in Europe in the early 15th century, and so Europeans generally used honey as a sweetener. It was not possible to grow sugar cane economically in Europe, but it could be successfully raised on the Azores and Canary Islands in the Atlantic Ocean, which the Spanish and Portuguese occupied at the end of the 15th century. The sugar plantations that were established on these islands were hugely profitable because they were worked by slaves. At first the Europeans enslaved the native population of the islands to work the plantations. Then, when so many islanders had died that they had become virtually extinct, the Europeans brought in slaves from west Africa.

Above: Farm workers shearing sheep. Fleeces from sheep were in great demand to make woolen cloth—but land fenced in to keep sheep meant many peasants lost their homes.

SEE ALSO

♦ Daily Life
♦ Food and Drink
♦ Poverty
♦ Trade

towns or starved. There was a great deal of peasant unrest during this era, ending in the Peasants' Revolt in Germany in 1525–1526.

However, some peasants prospered from these changed conditions and turned their labor services into money

Peasants were thrown out of their ancestral manors to make way for sheep

rents. Sometimes the lord of the manor fell into debt and was forced to sell his estate to a rich merchant, who might divide it into specialized units of production. By 1600 farmers were producing many profitable crops and sending them for sale in distant markets.

In the milder climates of the Mediterranean lighter woolen garments were highly prized. In Spain Moreno sheep produced a fine fiber that was suitable for the climate of the south. Spanish wool was transported to central Italy, where weavers turned it into beautiful fabrics.

The sheep that produced this wool were raised by a system known as transhumance, in which the animals were driven over great distances from summer to winter pastures and back again. However, transhumance did not mix well with traditional farming, because the herds of animals on the move consumed and trampled crops. Because wool was more profitable than the traditional growing of grains, grain farming declined in Spain, as it did in other parts of Europe. In the kingdom of Castile the monarchy favored large-scale herding, which conquistadors eventually introduced in the Americas.

the case of sheep, for their wool. In the damp cold of northern Europe woolen fabrics were in great demand. Sheep raised in England, Scotland, and Wales produced fleeces that were both warm and waterproof. Raw wool from these regions was shipped to manufacturing centers in Belgium, where it was turned into fine fabrics by skilled workers.

LAND FENCED IN

In England and Germany a great deal of land was fenced in (enclosed) by rich landowners for sheep grazing. The new enclosure laws meant that peasants and tenant-farmers were thrown out of their ancestral manors to make way for sheep. Some became sharecroppers or landless laborers. Others drifted to the

Alberti

Leon Battista Alberti (1404–1472) was a churchman with a passionate interest in the progress of art and architecture, and it is for his work in these fields that he is famous. He sought to revive the values of classical (ancient Roman and Greek) art and wrote books to guide painters, sculptors, and architects in the pursuit of this aim. His interests were wide-ranging—he also wrote important works on family life and geography—and historians consider him one of the first "Renaissance" or "universal" men, that is, a man who excels in many areas of learning.

Alberti was born to a wealthy banking family in Genoa and studied civil and canon (church) law at Bologna University. Like many educated people of his time, Alberti became interested in humanism, a new branch of learning based on the study of ancient Greek and Roman writers. After he finished his degree, Alberti worked as a papal secretary in Rome and later became a prior in Florence. He also devoted much time to writing about the arts and to designing buildings, and these works had a great influence on later architects. While in Florence he became friendly with many leading artists of the time, including Brunelleschi, Donatello, Ghiberti, and Masaccio.

He encouraged painters and sculptors who were seeking to make their work look more naturalistic, or real-looking, and who, along with architects, were interested in imitating the appearance of Roman art and architecture. In 1436 he wrote a treatise (a type of book) on the theory and practice of painting that gave the first description of perspective, the mathematical system that enabled artists to create the illusion of space in their pictures. He also wrote a treatise for sculptors in about 1464.

ARCHITECTURAL WORK

Alberti's first major architectural commission came from Sigismondo Malatesta, lord of Rimini, who asked him to redesign a medieval church in the classical style to house his tomb.

Above: Alberti designed this palace in Florence for the wealthy Rucellai family in the late 1440s. It is based on his study of Roman ruins, especially the Colosseum in Rome, and influenced generations of later architects.

SANTA MARIA NOVELLA, FLORENCE

The new façade (front) that Alberti designed to screen the medieval church of Santa Maria Novella in Florence (begun in 1458) became one of his most influential works. He used elements from classical architecture such as the columns and the top portion with its triangular top, which is based on the front (known as the portico) of classical temples.

Alberti also used a simple system of proportion in order to achieve harmony, or balance, which was an important aim of Renaissance architects. The whole façade fits into a square shape. It also consists of three smaller squares equal in size—one on either side of the door and one with the triangular top. Alberti used two large scroll shapes to mask the roof of the church behind and link the upper and lower sections.

Alberti's façade provided other architects with an example of how to design a fashionable classical screen to disguise old churches and was much copied. He developed his ideas in two later churches he designed in Mantua, San Sebastiano (begun 1460) and San Andrea (designed 1470).

Above: The classical façade that Alberti designed for the church of Santa Maria Novella in Florence.

Alberti based his design (begun in 1446) on a famous Roman triumphal arch in Rimini. Triumphal arches were large monuments built by the Romans to celebrate great victories and leaders; so, by applying the design to Malatesta's church, Alberti was emphasizing Sigismondo's greatness.

At about the same time, Alberti also began work on two buildings for the wealthy Rucellai family in Florence. One of these projects was the redesign of a medieval church called Santa Maria Novella (see box), and the other was the design of a palace, the Palazzo Rucellai (built about 1445–1451). This building became very influential because it was the first palace in which the classical orders were used. The orders were the different columns that the Romans and Greeks built with and the system of rules (or orders)

governing their use. Alberti used pilasters (strips that look like flattened columns) and based his design on the Colosseum in Rome.

ARCHITECTURAL THEORIES

Alberti also wrote about how the rules of ancient Greek and Roman architecture could be applied to modern buildings in a treatise entitled *De re aedificatoria* ("On Architecture"). He began writing his treatise in the 1440s, and it was published after his death in 1485. *De re aedificatoria* was based on a treatise by a Roman architect called Vitruvius and also on Alberti's study of ancient monuments. It discussed various subjects including mathematics, engineering, history, and town planning, and reflected the wide knowledge that came to be expected of Renaissance architects.

Alchemy

The term "alchemy" was coined in the 12th century to describe the field of activity devoted to finding a way of transforming base metals like copper and lead into gold. Alchemists hoped to discover a substance—called the elixir of life—that would not only transform metals but would also cure illnesses and make people live for ever. Although their work is now viewed as magic, in the Renaissance it was considered a legitimate branch of science, or natural philosophy.

Alchemy became popular in the countries of western Europe from the 12th and 13th centuries, when many Greek and Arabic books were translated into Latin. These books included descriptions of how base metals could be turned into gold. The most influential were by the Greek alchemist Xosimos of Panopolis (about

Above: A 16th-century painting of an alchemist and his assistants in their laboratory.

the third century A.D.) and the Arabic alchemist ar-Razi (about 850–923). Their writings stimulated alchemists in the West to search for the process that would be the key to unlimited wealth—a quest pursued with zeal throughout the 15th and 16th centuries.

BELIEFS ABOUT THE WORLD

Medieval and Renaissance alchemists based their search on certain beliefs about the world and the universe. Their ideas were founded on the writings of the Greek philosopher Aristotle (384–322 B.C.), whose theories had been kept alive by Arabic scholars such as Avicenna (980–1037 A.D.) and Averröes (1126–1198). They believed that everything in the world was made from the same basic matter, and that matter consisted of four elements: earth, water, fire, and air. So, argued the alchemists, it should be possible

THE ALCHEMIST

Alchemists were often seen as swindlers who tried to trick people into giving them money in return for making gold. In popular literature, from Chaucer's *Canterbury Tales* (1387) to Ben Jonson's play *The Alchemist* (1610), they were portrayed as crooks and their victims as gullible fools. However, many alchemists were highly regarded by rulers, who were attracted by the idea of limitless riches and eternal life, and alchemists were hired to work in princely courts across Europe. Prague in Bohemia (present-day Czech Republic) was known as "the metropolis of alchemy," and the Holy Roman emperors Maximilian II (ruled 1564–1576) and Rudolf II (ruled 1576–1612) encouraged leading alchemists such as the Englishman John Dee (1527–1608) to come to their court there.

Many alchemists believed that if they found a substance capable of turning base metals to gold, it would also be a cure for all illnesses and would

---

By making chemical drugs, alchemists had a great influence on the development of modern medicine

---

make people immortal. Although they were never to discover such a substance, alchemists did begin making medicines from minerals and chemicals—previously physicians had used only medicines made from plants.

PARACELSUS AND MEDICINES

By making chemical drugs, alchemists had a great influence on the development of modern medicine. The Swiss alchemist and physician Paracelsus (1493–1541) was the first doctor to use chemically made medicines; he also urged other doctors to experiment and find out for themselves which cures worked, rather than simply accepting ancient theories.

Some alchemists, such as the Frenchman Nicholas Flamel (1330–1418), claimed to have succeeded in turning base metals into gold and finding a "universal cure," but they shrouded their methods in great secrecy. Despite constant failure alchemists continued to try to find ways of making gold into the 18th century, and their experiments with chemical and mineral substances eventually became what we call chemistry today. Not until the 19th century was the possibility of making gold using chemicals conclusively disproved.

Above: A picture of the sun from the Splendor Solis, a 16th-century book about alchemy.

SEE ALSO

♦ Astrology
♦ Magic and Superstition
♦ Medicine and Surgery
♦ Science

to change one substance into another by manipulating the elements that they were composed of. In order to do this, alchemists developed special apparatus and processes.

A MAGICAL ELIXIR

Alchemists were convinced they could discover an elixir (special substance) that would be capable of changing matter. During the course of their experiments alchemists discovered how to make alcoholic spirits and mineral acids (acids made from rocks)—nitric, sulfuric, and hydrochloric acid.

Alexander VI

Pope Alexander VI (1431–1503) was one of the most powerful and influential figures of late 15th-century Italy. A wealthy and shrewd leader, he was also a great patron of the arts and continued the efforts made by earlier popes to turn Rome into a city of beauty and culture.

Alexander was born Rodrigo Borgia in Spain in the year 1431. He was a member of the powerful Borgia family, and his career was greatly helped by his uncle Alfonso Borgia. When Rodrigo was a teenager, Alfonso was a cardinal (a leading official of the Catholic church). Alfonso paid for Rodrigo's education in Rome and Bologna, where Rodrigo studied church law.

In 1455 Alfonso became Pope Calixtus III. The following year, when Rodrigo was 24, Alfonso made him a cardinal. In 1457 Rodrigo's meteoric rise continued when he was appointed vice-chancellor of the Roman church.

WINNING THE PAPACY

When Pope Innocent VIII died, Rodrigo became a contender for the papal throne. Although he was not a favored candidate, he won and was proclaimed Pope Alexander VI on August 11, 1492. The people of Rome welcomed the new pope with enthusiasm even though there were rumors that only Alexander's wealth and powerful connections had made his narrow victory possible.

Once he was pope, Alexander ruled in a fashion more befitting a prince than a religious leader. His taste for women and displays of wealth became infamous. Priests were supposed to be chaste and live as humbly as possible, so Alexander's behavior caused a great deal of resentment.

Alexander had considerable skills as an administrator. He restored law and order in Rome and reformed the papal finances. He also proved to be a capable politician and played a significant role in the Italian Wars that began when the French king Charles VIII entered Italy

Above: A portrait of Pope Alexander VI, who was a member of the powerful Borgia family. As pope he ruled like a Renaissance prince.

with a large army in September 1494. Bringing together Venice, Milan, the king of Spain, and the Holy Roman emperor, Alexander created the powerful "Holy Alliance" (also called the League of Venice), which managed to expel Charles from Italy.

THE TREATY OF TORDESILLAS

Alexander was responsible for the church becoming involved in the colonization of the New World. Following Columbus's discovery of the West Indies in 1492, Spain and Portugal became engaged in fierce competition for the new territories. Alexander was asked by the king and queen of Spain to act as arbitrator, and his negotiations led to the signing of the Treaty of Tordesillas in 1494. This treaty divided the New World in half. All lands lying west of an imaginary line that was drawn about 1,100 miles (1,770km) west of the Cape Verde Islands went to Spain, and everything to the east of the line went to Portugal.

Alexander's accomplishments were overshadowed by his corruption, however. Before he became pope, Alexander had fathered at

Below: The Castel Sant'Angelo in Rome, which was restored by Alexander VI.

least seven children. Four of them—Cesare, Juan, Jofré, and Lucrezia—were the result of his long affair with a Roman noblewoman, Vanozza Catanei. Throughout his life Alexander was always fiercely devoted to his children and focused his immense energies on making the Borgia family more powerful. He secured favorable marriages for his children, gave them lands belonging to Roman barons he exiled, and initiated battles in order to acquire territory for them.

The most famous of Alexander's children was Cesare Borgia. With the support of his father Cesare conquered the duchies of Emilia, Umbria, and Romagna. Cesare's cunning and brutality were so admired by Niccolò Machiavelli that he immortalized Cesare's activities in his political treatise *The Prince*.

Alexander was also a major patron of the arts. Under his guidance the Castel Sant'Angelo (an ancient fortress in the Vatican) was restored, and the University of Rome was rebuilt. He also commissioned the artist Pinturicchio to decorate the Castel and the Vatican apartments with frescoes.

Americas

The "New World" that the Europeans claimed to have "discovered" at the end of the 15th century was already home to between 60 and 80 million Native Americans. Some of these people lived in small communities, while others lived in large, highly developed societies.

The largest Native American societies were those of the Aztecs and the Incas. In central Mexico the Aztecs ruled an empire of 30 million people from their capital city, Tenochtitlán. Aztec society consisted of nobles and commoners. The nobles filled offices of civil, military, and religious authority, while the commoners were farmers, craftsmen, soldiers, and merchants. Aztec farmers raised crops such as corn and beans but had no animals other than turkeys and small dogs. Aztec craftsmen practiced a wide range of skills, such as bricklaying, goldsmithing, and basketmaking. Merchants helped distribute goods by buying and selling products in great open markets and carrying out long-distance trade.

In addition to the food and goods they produced themselves, the Aztecs received tribute from tribes they had conquered. These conquered peoples also had to send large numbers of captives to the Aztecs regularly, to be sacrificed to their gods.

THE INCA EMPIRE

In South America the most powerful Native Americans were the Incas. From their capital in Cuzco, in what is now Peru, the Incas controlled an empire of several million people stretching from present-day Ecuador to Chile and connected by 12,500 miles (20,000km) of royal highways. Most of its people lived in the mountains and high valleys

Above: Hernán Cortés being greeted by the Aztec king Montezuma in Tenochtitlán.

NEW SPAIN
Havana · CUBA
Mexico ·
HISPANIOLA
PUERTO RICO
JAMAICA
Guatemala ·
Portobello
Panama ·
· Santa Fe
Atlantic Ocean
PERU
Pacific Ocean
BRAZIL
Lima · · Cuzco
· Potosí
Buenos Aires

Spanish colonies

Portuguese colonies

to cruise along the coasts, explore the bays and rivers, and lay claim to new lands. After the explorers came the settlers. The Spanish, Portuguese, French, and English all tried to set up colonies in the Americas. However, only the Spanish and Portuguese were successful in establishing permanent colonies during the 16th century.

A NEW SPANISH EMPIRE

The Spanish were the first to lay claim to large tracts of the New World. Between 1492 and 1520 Spanish soldiers conquered the Caribbean. Then, between 1519 and 1540 they conquered the Aztec and Inca empires. They set up settlements and by 1600 had established a Spanish empire that extended from what is now the southern United States south to Chile.

The Spanish invasion was led by conquistadors—private soldiers who were authorized by the Spanish crown. The conquistadors were able to conquer Native American armies that vastly outnumbered them because the Spanish had horses and guns. They also had metal armor, which made them

of the Andes, where they raised crops such as corn and potatoes and kept llamas as pack animals.

Above: The extent of the Spanish and Portuguese colonies in the Americas in 1580.

VILLAGE LIFE

In North America Native American tribes had a simpler lifestyle. Some lived in villages or a group of villages governed by a council or by a chief who ruled in consultation with his people. Some villages were permanent and were surrounded by farmland. Other tribespeople lived in temporary camps, moving around in search of food. In most of South America life was even simpler. Some people lived in small villages and practiced limited farming, while others moved around constantly, collecting food by hunting, gathering, and fishing.

After Christopher Columbus's pioneering voyage in 1492 many other explorers soon arrived in the Americas

THE AZTEC CAPITAL

When the conquistador Hernán Cortés led his Spanish army into Tenochtitlán, the Aztec capital, he found a city as large and complex as any in Europe. It was home to more than 200,000 people and was the center of Aztec government and religion. As Cortés recorded, Aztec nobles lived in the city's "very fine houses" with "flower gardens of every kind." In the center of the city were great palaces for royal officials and pyramid-shaped temples, one of which, according to Cortés, was large enough to hold a town of 15,000 inside its walls. The real heart of the city, though, was its public markets. Tenochtitlán's largest market was "twice as big as that of Salamanca [in Spain] and was completely surrounded by arcades where there are daily more than 60,000 folk buying and selling."

almost invulnerable to the Native Americans' wooden and stone weapons, and metal swords and pikes. The conquistadors were also able to gather allies from the peoples that had been conquered by the Aztecs and Incas. Another very important factor in the Spaniards' success was the devastating effect of diseases such as smallpox that the invaders brought with them.

COLONIAL RULE

Once the Spanish had conquered an area, they colonized it. They established their own form of government that allowed the Spanish king to supervise his colonies from Spain. Colonists were supposed to live in Spanish-style towns, each with a mayor and a town council to govern it. The region was divided into provinces, each with a royal governor and an *audienca*, a kind of council and supreme court. The provinces were organized into two viceroyalties—New Spain (Mexico) and Peru, each of which had a viceroy appointed by the king to run it. To make sure that all these officials did their jobs correctly, the king also appointed special inspectors who came to America to investigate the viceroys, the governors, and the *audiencas* to make sure they were following the king's instructions.

By 1550 perhaps 100,000 Spaniards had emigrated to America. Native Americans still outnumbered the Spanish, though their numbers were

Above: The Spanish defeating and capturing Native Americans after landing in Yucatán. The weapons and armor of the Native Americans were no match for those of the Spanish forces, who had guns, horses, swords, and metal body armor.

FRENCH AND ENGLISH COLONIES

France and England both tried and failed to establish colonies in the New World. The French set up a small base just north of Florida in 1562, but the Spanish soon attacked and destroyed it. The English tried further north, on what is now the coast of North Carolina. Between 1585 and 1587 Walter Raleigh tried three times to set up a colony on Roanoke Island. None of the three was very large, but the last one was large enough to worry Spain. Before the Spanish could find and attack the colony, however, it had disappeared. When relief ships arrived from England in 1590, they found the settlement abandoned. No one knows for sure what happened to "The Lost Colony." Some historians think the English colonists found refuge with friendly Native Americans when their supplies ran low. They may have remained in a Native American village until the last survivors were killed by other tribespeople in the early 17th century.

falling fast as they died from the diseases that the Spanish brought with them. The Spanish also brought African slaves to work for them. The result was a very mixed but very structured society. At the top were the rich descendants of the original conquistadors and early settlers who had made their fortunes in America. Members of this elite were proud of their Spanish blood and tried to live as people did in Spain. Beneath them were the poorer Spaniards, the Native Americans, African slaves, and people of mixed race.

Below: Spanish overseers punishing Native American workers in a silver mine. After Spanish rule was established, the local people were forced to work on farms or in mines, often under very harsh conditions.

By the 1540s the Spanish crown had condemned the practice of slavery. However, Native Americans were required to work on Spanish farms or in mines, in return for which they would receive military protection and training in the Catholic faith. Legally, this was not slavery since they were supposed to be free, but it was hard to tell the difference.

PORTUGUESE COLONIES

The only other kingdom to colonize the Americas successfully in the 16th century was Portugal. In 1500 a Portuguese fleet bound for India drifted off course and landed in Brazil, which was claimed for Portugal. The Portuguese soon returned and set up fortified warehouses to trade with the Native Americans. In 1530 the Portuguese king decided to establish permanent colonies in Brazil, and 12 captains received royal grants to all the land of Brazil.

Each captain was given the right to appoint local officials, establish towns, and grant land to settlers. Each captain also kept some of the land for himself on which he could set up highly profitable sugar plantations. It was difficult to attract settlers, though, and

some of the captains gave up the struggle and returned home. Others enslaved Native Americans to work on their plantations, and this led to Native American revolts that very nearly destroyed the colony.

In 1548 the Portuguese crown established royal government in Brazil to protect the colony, and African slaves were shipped in to provide labor for the plantations. By 1600 there were about 30,000 Portuguese and 20,000 Africans living in Brazil.

THE AMERICAS' EFFECT ON EUROPE

The economic effect of the Americas on Europe was enormous. Gold and silver poured into Spain from captured Aztec and Inca treasures and from new silver mines. By 1600, 25,000 tons (23,000 tonnes) of American silver had arrived in Spain. Most of it went on to other European countries to pay for goods bought by Spain or to repay loans made to the Spanish king to pay for Spanish wars. This great influx of silver caused inflation. By 1600 prices all over Europe were rising, making it harder for ordinary people to pay for food and clothing.

The discovery of the Americas gave the countries of western Europe new lands to conquer at a time when expansion to the east was blocked by the might of the Ottoman Empire. However, it also gave them new reasons to fight one another. French and English ships raided Spanish and Portuguese colonies and tried to capture the Spanish treasure fleets as they crossed the Atlantic. This was one of the reasons why King Philip II of Spain sent his Armada to try to invade England in 1588.

Above: The remains of a Spanish hacienda (ranchhouse) built during the early colonial period. The Spanish crown decreed that colonists should build Spanish-style houses and towns in the Americas.

SEE ALSO
♦ Elizabeth I
♦ Exploration
♦ Portugal
♦ Spain

Anatomy

Along with all the other things that were being newly studied in the Renaissance was the human body. Very little was known in the Middle Ages about how the body worked, since the cutting up (dissection) of corpses was strictly forbidden by the church. Much of what was known came from the writings of the second-century Greek physician Galen.

Galen emphasized that it was essential for anyone practicing medicine to have a good knowledge of human anatomy. His own knowledge was based on the works of the earlier Greek physicians Herophilus and Erasistratus, both of whom had dissected human bodies. But Galen himself had only cut up dogs, monkeys, pigs, sheep, and goats. He made some important discoveries, such as the valves of the heart and the difference between veins and arteries, but his books also included many errors, which were repeated and elaborated by medieval writers. Although from the 13th century onward a few universities in Italy and France did permit some dissections of human bodies for teaching purposes, nobody had dared challenge Galen's assertions.

LEARNING BY EXPERIENCE

With the Renaissance, however, came a new way of thinking that encouraged people to learn things by experience— to explore, to test, to discover. The taboos against cutting up dead bodies were gradually lifted, and the practice

Left: A 16th-century painting of an anatomy lesson for artists. A body is being dissected while the students make drawings and take notes.

LEONARDO'S ANATOMICAL DRAWINGS

Leonardo da Vinci worked on his anatomical drawings over a period of many years. Based on his own dissections of human bodies, the extraordinarily detailed and accurate drawings were to form the basis of much later scientific illustration. Leonardo called his drawings "demonstrations" of nature. They were better than any written description at conveying the valuable information distilled from Leonardo's many hours at the dissecting table. He was extremely proud of his anatomical notebooks and begged his students to make sure that they were published. He died in 1519 before he could complete the work.

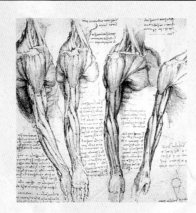

Left: A page from one of Leonardo's notebooks, showing his detailed drawings of the muscles of the arm and the shoulder.

of dissection led to major discoveries from about 1500 onward.

Leonardo da Vinci was fascinated by the human body. He first began to study anatomy to improve his skills as an artist, but his researches on the skeleton and muscles led him to explore the structure and functions of the heart, lungs, and brain, and the digestive and reproductive systems. Leonardo personally dissected 30 bodies, mostly at the medical schools and teaching hospitals of Milan, Florence, Rome, and Pavia. He made a series of detailed anatomical drawings, with notes, which were the best representations of human anatomy that had ever been seen.

THE WORK OF ANDREAS VESALIUS

The first really comprehensive textbook of anatomy, however, was the work of Andreas Vesalius (1514–1564), a Flemish physician who studied at the universities of Louvain, Paris, and Padua. Padua was a progressive university, particularly in medicine and science, and was one of the first to allow dissection of human bodies by its teachers. In 1538, when Vesalius was appointed lecturer in surgery there, Galen's works were still the basis of anatomical studies throughout Europe.

Vesalius did dissections himself, instead of (as was more usual) leaving it to poorly trained assistants. He soon found that the anatomy of the bodies he dissected differed in significant details from that described by Galen. Vesalius prepared a complete textbook of human anatomy, containing both illustrations and a commentary, which was published in 1543 under the title *The Seven Books on the Structure of the Human Body.* This work described the skeleton, muscles, blood vessels, and the nervous and digestive systems. It became a crucial textbook for the study of medicine. It also showed that Galen's work included serious errors and could no longer be regarded as sound.

Later anatomists of the Renaissance continued to study how the body worked. In particular, the English physician William Harvey (1578–1657) investigated the way blood circulated in the body. His inquiries led him to conclude that the heart worked like a "water bellows" and pumped blood around the body.

SEE ALSO
♦ Leonardo da Vinci
♦ Medicine and Surgery

Angelico, Fra

Above: Fra Angelico painted this picture of the Annunciation *for the monastery of San Marco in 1450. It shows the moment when the angel Gabriel announces to Mary that she will give birth to Jesus.*

Fra Angelico (about 1400–1455) was one of the leading Italian painters of the first half of the 15th century. He lived and worked mainly in Florence and the nearby town of Fiesole, though he also received commissions in Orvieto, Perugia, and Rome. His paintings have religious subjects, and most were made for the Dominican Order, a religious brotherhood he entered in about 1420. Although his real name was Guido di Pietro, later historians gave him the name Fra Angelico, which means "the angelic brother," because of his devout life and the heavenly beauty of his paintings.

Among Fra Angelico's best-known works are a series of wall paintings in the Dominican monastery of San Marco in Florence, where he lived from 1439. Many show scenes from Christ's life. Each is painted with a limited range of colors and a simple arrangement, or composition, that focuses attention on the main event shown. Fra Angelico painted the scenes in this way to help the monks concentrate their thoughts on God, and his work reflects the ideas of Dominican reformers, who urged artists to adopt a clear style.

NEW ARTISTIC DEVELOPMENTS

Fra Angelico's paintings also show that he was aware of new artistic developments in Florence. Artists were eager to make their work look realistic, and one of the ways they tried to achieve this was by creating the illusion of space in their pictures. Fra Angelico created space in his paintings by arranging the figures carefully, often placing them in buildings or with views of landscapes in the background—while earlier artists had used flat gold backgrounds.

Fra Angelico also painted pictures with rich colors and many figures. Their more complex and showy appearance reflects their function, because many of them were painted as altarpieces (pictures placed behind altars in churches) that would be seen by many people. They were paid for by wealthy patrons such as Cosimo de Medici and Palla Strozzi, who would have wanted the paintings to reflect their wealth as well as their faith. Fra Angelico used the same clear style and graceful figures in all his work, and it is these qualities that continue to make his paintings popular.

Anguissola

The Italian painter Sofonisba Anguissola (about 1532–1625) was the first important woman artist of the Renaissance. Unlike other female painters of the time, such as Lavinia Fontana, she was not the daughter of an artist. Her father was a nobleman of Cremona who had six daughters, all of whom received a humanist education.

Along with her sisters Elena and Lucia, Sofonisba was tutored in painting and was soon doing portraits of local nobles as well as self-portraits. Among Anguissola's more unusual early works is a double portrait, which shows her instructor Bernardino Campi as he paints a picture of Anguissola.

Renaissance women artists often specialized in portraiture because women were barred from the art academies, where male students studied anatomy and did large-scale history paintings. Anguissola became skilled in portraying animated facial expressions, and her portraits contributed to the development of early baroque naturalism and genre painting, which emphasized the sitter's emotions and personality. Among her many admirers was the artist Michelangelo. The drawing she did at his request—*Boy Bitten by a Crayfish*—later inspired a similar work by the baroque artist Caravaggio.

THE SPANISH COURT

In 1559 Anguissola's fame brought her to the attention of King Philip II of Spain, who invited her to Madrid to serve as court painter and lady-in-waiting to Queen Isabel. Many of the paintings she did during her 14 years at the court were destroyed in a fire, but those that survived include formal portraits of Philip II and Isabel.

In 1573 Anguissola left Spain to marry a Sicilian nobleman, Don Fabrizio de Moncada. After his death in 1579 she married another nobleman, Orazio Lomellini, who was from Genoa. She continued to paint until failing eyesight forced her to retire. After Lomellini's death Anguissola moved to Palermo, where she opened a studio. She died in 1625, aged about 92.

Above: Sofonisba Anguissola's painting entitled Husband and Wife, *one of her many portraits.*

SEE ALSO

♦ Baroque
♦ Gentileschi
♦ Naturalism
♦ Portraiture
♦ Women

Antiquities

Antiquities are any objects made by humans that have survived from the distant past. In the Renaissance the term was used specifically to refer to the remains of ancient Roman civilization, which scholars, rulers, and artists viewed as a golden age of culture. Roman antiquities included the ruins of buildings, sculpture, coins, medals, gems, and mosaics. Wealthy men were eager to collect these objects, and architects, sculptors, and painters tried to imitate them in their work.

At its peak in the second century B.C. the Roman Empire stretched from North Africa in the south to Scotland in the north, and from Spain in the west to Persia in the east. It was prosperous, highly organized, and powerful, and was ruled from the flourishing city of Rome. However, the empire began to fall apart in the third century A.D. and in the fourth century A.D. was divided into two empires: the Eastern or Byzantine Empire, with its capital in Constantinople (present-day Istanbul), and the Western Empire, with its capital in Rome. Although the Eastern Empire prospered, the Western Empire (covering western Europe) declined, and its last emperor, Romulus Augustus, was overthrown by the Ostrogoth ruler Theodoric in 476.

IN THE MIDDLE AGES

Although the countries of western Europe were unstable and fragmented following the collapse of the Western Empire, signs of Roman civilization remained. The ruins of buildings and monuments such as temples, theaters, stadiums, baths, and triumphal arches were scattered throughout Europe. The greatest concentration of ruins was in

Above: An antique sarcophagus (stone coffin) with a carving showing Bacchus, the Roman god of wine (the standing male figure center right), and a group of revelers. Ariadne, whom Bacchus married, is shown reclining on the right of the group. Many antique sarcophaguses survived in the Renaissance and influenced artists.

Rome, although many were covered in wooded thickets and debris as the city became little more than a shantytown.

Roman antiquities were never entirely neglected in the Middle Ages. In the eighth century Charlemagne (742–814), king of the Franks, revived Roman culture at his court in Aachen, Germany. However, on the whole, medieval interest in antiquities was

> *In the 15th century artists began to study Roman antiquities systematically*

sporadic and consisted mainly of reusing Roman objects for practical purposes. Builders converted Roman structures to new uses or took their columns and blocks of stone for new buildings, and people often reused carved Roman sarcophaguses (stone coffins) for burials or for turning into baths or altars.

It was not until the 15th century that artists began to study Roman antiquities systematically. Their interest grew out of humanist scholars' study of great Roman writers. It was also stimulated by the rebuilding of Rome under the direction of the popes, which began in the mid-15th century. During work to clear the city of overgrowth and rubbish many ancient buildings and bits of sculpture were unearthed.

ANCIENT RUINS

The most obvious and imposing remains were ruined buildings. In Rome they included the Colosseum, the temples and government buildings of the Forum, huge complexes of Roman baths such as those of Diocletian, and triumphal arches like that of Constantine. Only one building had survived with its basic structure

MARCUS AURELIUS

The bronze statue of the Roman emperor Marcus Aurelius (ruled 161–180 A.D.) mounted on horseback was one of the most important Roman sculptures to survive to the Renaissance. In the Middle Ages it was thought to show Emperor Constantine (ruled 306–337 A.D.), the first Christian emperor. Had people known that it showed Marcus Aurelius, a pagan, they would probably have destroyed it. The statue was very influential in the Renaissance because it was a powerful way to portray a leader and allowed artists to show their skill in representing a horse. It was also a great technical feat—the massive weight of the sculpture was supported on just three of the horse's slender legs. Donatello's sculpture of *Gattamelata* (1447–1453) and Verrocchio's *Colleoni Monument* (1479–1488) were both based on the statue of Marcus Aurelius.

Right: The Roman sculpture of Marcus Aurelius. It was much admired in the Renaissance, when it was made the centerpiece of the Capitoline hill where Rome's government was based.

Left: The Pantheon in Rome was the only Roman building to survive intact into the Renaissance. It was built as a pagan temple but was converted into a Christian church in 609. The building was very influential in the Renaissance, and the famous artist Raphael was buried there.

intact: the Pantheon, a huge circular temple crowned with a dome and fronted by an open structure (a portico) consisting of columns supporting a carved triangular top (a pediment). Renaissance architects studied these monuments and incorporated many of the features they saw into their own designs and theories.

ANTIQUE SCULPTURE

With buildings sculptures were the most influential antiquities. Although many had been broken or burned to make lime for building, a large number remained. They were of two sorts: relief sculptures (carvings on a background panel) and sculptures in the round, which stand freely with no background.

Relief sculptures were most common because they often decorated large objects that could not easily be broken or burned. They decorated sarcophaguses, monuments—such as triumphal arches and columns celebrating great Roman leaders and their victories—and architecture, especially pediments. The subject matter of relief sculptures was often drawn from myth or showed scenes of Roman life or of events the sculptures commemorated.

Much less sculpture in the round survived because it was more delicate and could easily be carried away and burned. The few examples that were known were figure sculptures showing Roman gods and mythical figures, as well as portraits. They were particularly influential as Renaissance artists sought to make their work look more lifelike and concentrated on portraying the human body.

The three most important antique sculptures known in the Renaissance were the *Apollo Belvedere*, the *Belvedere Torso*, and the *Laocoön*. The first two were unearthed in the 15th century—although the exact dates of their discovery are unknown—and the *Laocoön* was dug up in 1506.

The *Apollo Belvedere* shows the god Apollo, who represented the values of civilized life, particularly music. He is portrayed as a handsome, graceful young man, and for centuries artists regarded the statue as the perfect portrayal of youthful male beauty. The *Belvedere Torso* is just a fragment of an antique sculpture. The arms and legs are missing, leaving the trunk (torso) of a heavily built, muscular man. It was much praised for the way it conveyed muscular strength and movement, as was the *Laocoön* (see box on page 30).

Because paintings are even more delicate than sculptures, virtually none survived from Roman times. Most of what Renaissance artists knew about Roman pictures came from descriptions in the work of Roman writers such as Pliny the Elder (23–79 A.D.) and from mosaic floors (floors with designs made from differently colored pieces of marble and stone) that hinted at developments in painting.

The most exciting discovery for painters was Nero's Golden House, a huge palace complex built for the Emperor Nero in 65–68 A.D. In the late 15th century parts of the site were excavated, and decorations were found on the walls of underground rooms called grottoes. These decorations featured gracefully interlinked motifs of flowers, plants, human figures, and real and imaginary animals. This kind of decoration—known as "grotesque" after the grottoes in which it was discovered—became very fashionable in the 16th century.

RENAISSANCE COLLECTIONS

As interest in the Roman world increased in the 15th century, it became fashionable to collect antiquities as a sign of learning, wealth, and power. Many artists and scholars owned fragments of Roman sculpture, but only rich rulers and popes could afford larger and more choice pieces.

Below: A 16th-century drawing of an artist studying the ancient Roman sculpture known as the Laocoön. *The statue was in the papal collection of antique sculptures that was displayed in the Belvedere Courtyard of the Vatican, Rome.*

THE LAOCOÖN

The *Laocoön* was discovered in Rome in January 1506, and scholars immediately recognized that it was a sculpture vividly described by the Roman writer Pliny the Elder, who considered it one of the greatest works of art in the world. The marble sculpture shows an incident from the story of the Trojan War. After failing to capture the city of Troy by force, the Greeks pretended to sail home, leaving an enormous wooden horse outside the gates. Laocoön, a Trojan priest, warned his fellow citizens not to bring the horse into the city, but they ignored him, and the Greek soldiers hidden inside it brought about the destruction of Troy. The Greek gods cruelly punished Laocoön for trying to spoil their plan and sent serpents to crush him and his two sons to death.

Right: The sculpture Laocoön, *which influenced Renaissance artists like Michelangelo who were impressed by its sense of drama and movement.*

Lorenzo de Medici (1449–1492), the head of the most powerful family in Florence, amassed a large and varied collection of ancient objects. It included not only sculpture, but also coins, vases, gems with designs cut in them, and cameos (portraits or miniature designs cut on small pieces of hard stone). Lorenzo displayed some of his sculpture in his garden and allowed promising young artists to study there, including Michelangelo.

From the time of Pope Paul II (pope 1464–1471) the papacy assembled the greatest collection of antiquities. Pope Julius II (pope 1503–1513) displayed many of these sculptures in the Belvedere Courtyard in the Vatican. They included the *Laocoön* and the *Apollo Belvedere* and *Belvedere Torso* (both named after the courtyard). Pope Sixtus IV (pope 1471–1484) also presented a collection of antiquities to the citizens of Rome. This collection was housed in a museum on the Capitoline hill on which the Renaissance government of Rome was based.

INFLUENCE OF ANTIQUITIES

These antiquities were very influential in the Renaissance, and many artists traveled to Rome in order to study them. Even if artists were unable to see them firsthand, they could study them in the form of plaster casts and copies made from the originals. A huge trade grew up in the manufacture of these copies and many wealthy men and artists' workshops owned collections of them. Workshops usually also had sketchbooks full of drawings of antique sculptures, and from the mid-16th century advances in printing and cheaper paper meant that prints illustrating many antiquities, including buildings, were widely available.

Antwerp

Renaissance Antwerp was the great boom town of northern Europe. Its position on the navigable Schelde River made it a natural port, and by the close of the 14th century it was a thriving international market-place with a population of about 20,000 people. In the next 50 years this population quadrupled, and it quickly overtook its rival Bruges, becoming the biggest and wealthiest city in northern Europe.

The main business of Antwerp was the processing, finishing, and selling of woolen cloth. Other industries included silk factories, tapestry weaving, sugar refineries, and the beginnings of a diamond trade. There were also breweries, malt factories, bleaching and dyeing plants, and finance—Antwerp had its own stock exchange by 1531, before either London or Amsterdam.

A CENTER OF CULTURE

Antwerp also developed a vigorous intellectual and cultural life. Printing was one of the new industries, and with master printers and engravers came artists, writers, philosophers, and radicals. The city became an important center of the Protestant movement. Artists thrived in Antwerp, and it had its own school of painting, led by Pieter Bruegel the Elder and his sons. In the mid-16th century Antwerp was described by a visitor from Florence as the loveliest city in the world.

The great economic boom was not to last. Bankruptcies and religious intolerance contributed to a decline. Antwerp and much of its surrounding provinces were governed by Spain at this time, and the Catholic Spanish king was determined to persecute

---

In the mid-16th century Antwerp was described by a visitor from Florence as the loveliest city in the world

---

Protestants. Antwerp joined a league of Flemish cities opposed to Spanish rule. When war broke out, control of Antwerp became crucial. The city was besieged and captured in 1585 by the Duke of Parma. In response the league closed the Schelde River to shipping, but the consequences for commerce in the city were disastrous. In the next four years half the population left and moved their businesses to other cities.

Above: The bourse (stock exchange) of Antwerp, which was established in 1531. A stock exchange was a place where merchants and dealers met to trade bonds and other types of securities.

SEE ALSO

♦ Bruegel, Pieter the Elder
♦ Bruges
♦ Trade

Architecture

Architecture is the name given to the art and technology of building, as well as to the buildings produced, and usually applies to large, important structures such as churches, cathedrals, palaces, and town halls. Architecture has always varied according to different countries, climates, and building materials, and in response to changes in society and culture. Such changes began to take place in early 15th-century Italy and were reflected in the new buildings designed there.

From the 11th century new building increased across the countries of western Europe as a result of a more stable society, increased wealth from trade, and religious reforms. Because religion dominated life at that time, many of the new buildings were cathedrals. They were breathtakingly tall buildings with pointed arches, large stained-glass windows, slender columns, and lofty spires. The style in which they were built is known as the Gothic and was also used for other buildings such as town halls and houses. Buildings in the Gothic style continued to be put up throughout the 15th century: Milan Cathedral in Italy is a famous example.

NEW CLIENTS AND IDEAS

A new style of architecture began to emerge in the Italian city-state of Florence at the beginning of the 15th century. Florence was ruled not by landed lords or kings, but by a government elected from wealthy merchants and bankers. These self-made men saw architecture as the most impressive and enduring way to display their newly acquired power and wealth.

Ruins of ancient Roman buildings survived in great numbers throughout Italy, and even during the Middle Ages they had been regarded as reminders of a superior civilization. The merchants of Florence realized that a good way to emphasize their prosperity and authority would be to commission buildings in the ancient Roman style.

Above: This 16th-century painting in the ducal palace in Urbino, Italy, shows a view of an ideal Renaissance city. Palaces and public buildings with classical features such as columns surround a square, at the center of which stands a circular building.

Architects began to study the ruins, which included temples, triumphal arches, amphitheaters, and baths, and in Rome the Forum and Colosseum. Architects recorded these ruins in careful drawings and copied many of their features in their own buildings.

NEW PRINCIPLES

The basic difference between the Gothic style of medieval Europe and the classical style that emerged in 15th century Italy was the way the buildings were constructed. Gothic buildings were constructed using pointed arches, while classical buildings were built using rounded arches and upright posts supporting horizontal beams (a system known as post-and-beam). This

Below: A sheet of drawings showing a survey of the ruins of Diocletian's Baths in Rome by the architect Antonio da Sangallo the Elder (1455–1534). Many Renaissance architects studied Roman ruins.

was the system the ancient Greeks and Romans had used.

While medieval builders had sought to make their cathedrals as tall as possible, reaching up toward the heavens in praise of God, Renaissance architects were more concerned with designing harmonious, symmetrical, and geometrically ordered buildings. This change was partly based on their

---

Architects began to study Roman ruins and copied many of the features they saw in their own buildings

---

study of Roman ruins and partly on a book by a Roman architect called Vitruvius, who lived in the first century B.C. It also reflected the desire of humanist scholars and scientists to understand the order that lay behind appearances in the world.

Humanist scholars revived theories about harmony and geometry based on the study of classical authors such as Pythagoras (about 580–500 B.C.) and Plato (about 427–347 B.C.). They believed that musical harmony could be expressed in terms of mathematical ratios, and that certain shapes, such as the circle and square, were ideal, or perfect. In the Renaissance architects developed these ideas on harmony and applied them to their buildings.

RENAISSANCE CHURCHES

Despite its more humanist outlook, Renaissance society continued to be dominated by religion, and churches remained the most important and frequently commissioned buildings. The construction of Saint Peter's in

Rome was a major architectural project that ran throughout the 16th century. It employed leading architects of the day such as Raphael and Michelangelo (in the Renaissance professions were not as specialized as today, and many artists were also architects).

COLUMNS AND CLASSICAL MODELS

The appearance of Renaissance churches differed considerably from earlier Gothic ones. The most obvious change was the use of columns and the classical orders (see box). Often the façade (front) of the church was modeled on classical structures such as temple fronts or triumphal arches. Temple fronts stood on a base and had large columns supporting a low triangular gable called a pediment. Triumphal arches were big monuments built by the Romans to celebrate great victories or leaders. Two of Alberti's churches were modeled on triumphal arches: the Tempio Malatestiano in Rimini (built about 1446) and San Andrea in Mantua (designed 1470).

The layout of churches also reflected Renaissance ideas on harmony and geometry. Architects often based their designs on circles and squares (or spheres and cubes) because they were considered the most beautiful shapes.

Domes became popular to crown churches rather than the tall towers and spires that characterized Gothic churches. The dome of Florence Cathedral (begun 1418) designed by Filippo Brunelleschi is generally regarded as the first piece of Renaissance architecture, and the challenge of how to build the huge dome at Saint Peter's in Rome occupied several generations of architects.

Left: The church of Il Redentore (the Redeemer) in Venice, designed by Palladio in 1576 to mark the end of a terrible outbreak of the plague. With its large dome and façade based on temple fronts, it is a typical Renaissance church.

While earlier churches in western Europe had plans based on a Latin cross—a cross-shape in which one arm is longer than the other three—Renaissance architects often tried to fit their ground plans inside a square or circle and make all the arms of the cross the same length. They also built a dome above the central area of the church. Churches of this type are known as centrally planned or Greek-cross churches. They are called Greek-cross churches because this type of design had always been used in Greek Orthodox churches, although it had died out in Roman Catholic churches in the Middle Ages.

PALACES FOR THE RICH

Designing homes for wealthy families also kept architects busy. In cities they built palaces (*palazzi* in Italian) that often took up whole city blocks and

Left: The imposing Palazzo Medici in Florence, designed by Michelozzo in 1444. It has roughly shaped stonework (called rustication) to make it look strong, regular doors and windows, and an overhanging roof to provide shade from the hot sun.

THE CLASSICAL ORDERS

The classical orders are the columns used in classical architecture and the rules (orders) governing their use. In the Renaissance there were five different sorts of column: the Tuscan, Doric, Ionic, Corinthian, and Composite (later architects sometimes added more). The first four are based on columns written about by the Roman architect Vitruvius, while the Composite is a Renaissance invention. The easiest way to identify the different orders is to look at the top of the column (the capital). Tuscan and Doric capitals are plain—the way to tell them apart is to look higher, to the horizontal band above the capital called the frieze. The Doric frieze is carved with blocks of three vertical strips (called triglyphs), while the Tuscan is plain. The Ionic capital has scrolls like rams' horns, the Corinthian capital is carved with the leaves of the acanthus plant, and the Composite combines the decoration of the Ionic and Corinthian. Strict rules determined the proportions of the different columns, as well as the sort of buildings each should be used for.

Above: A drawing of the five classical orders used in the Renaissance. From left to right they are: the Tuscan, Doric, Ionic, Corinthian, and Composite.

THE BUILDING SITE

The Renaissance building site was run by a mason (builder) working to the instructions of an architect. The architect produced detailed drawings and models to show what the building should look like when it was finished, and visited the site regularly to check on progress. Important buildings were usually built of stone or marble—of which there were plentiful supplies in Italy—or of bricks covered with stucco (a type of plaster) to look like stone. On site, masons were the most important craftsmen. They finished shaping the stone that had been roughly cut to shape in the quarry and built the walls and ceilings. They made columns in cylinder-shaped sections that they then fitted together, and sculptors carved the capitals and other decorative details. Many other craftsmen were also involved, including bricklayers, mortar mixers, tilers, and blacksmiths, who made nails, bolts, and chains used to strengthen structures. Numerous unskilled laborers were also employed to help with all the hard work such as carrying building materials.

Above: A painting of the architect Brunelleschi showing a model of one of his designs to his patron.

sometimes required the demolition of many smaller buildings. The first floor of a palace was usually occupied by shops and storerooms. The main rooms for living and entertaining were located on the second floor, known as the *piano nobile* (Italian for "noble floor"), above the noise and smells of the street. Smaller rooms for servants were beneath the roof. Palaces were built around central courtyards to provide light and fresh air, with loggias (galleries) opening onto them.

Architects applied theories of harmony (concerning perfect shapes and ratios) and the classical orders (see box on page 35) to these buildings as they did to churches. Sometimes the outside walls of a palace did not have columns but were built with large, chunky-looking stones. This type of stonework is called rustication and was intended to make buildings look strong

and impenetrable. The palace designed in 1444 by Michelozzo for the Medici family in Florence is a good example. The classical orders were used for other palaces, such as Alberti's Palazzo Rucellai in Florence (late 1440s). The courtyard inside a palace was always surrounded by loggias fronted by classical columns.

COUNTRY VILLAS

Architects also designed country retreats and farms for wealthy city-dwellers. These buildings were different from traditional Italian farms, which were fortified. The new houses were based on what architects imagined ancient Roman villas (houses) had looked like. The most famous Renaissance villas were designed by Andrea Palladio in the countryside around Venice. His Villa Rotunda (about 1550) looks more like a Renaissance church than a house. It is centrally planned, topped by a dome, and surrounded by temple fronts—an ancient Roman villa would never have looked like this.

To design a building, Palladio took elements from different ancient Roman buildings and united them using Renaissance theories of harmony. He wrote a treatise on how classical architecture could be adapted to modern needs that became one of the most influential books on architecture.

PUBLIC BUILDINGS

New civic buildings were also designed by architects. Sansovino's library and mint (both begun 1537) on Saint Mark's Square in Venice and Palladio's town hall in Vicenza (1549) are just three examples. They all show the elaborate, sculptural classical style that developed in Venice from the 1530s.

Architects were also called on to design new fortifications around towns that would help protect them from the new cannon fire, against which old town walls were useless. The architect and military engineer Sanmicheli (1484–1559) is thought to have designed the new type of earthworks known as star bastions that were built to protect all major towns from the 16th century onward.

The greatest amount of new building took place in Rome from the mid-15th century, as the popes sought to restore the city to its ancient glory. The popes commissioned the

Below: The Campidoglio square on the Capitoline hill in Rome. It was redesigned with grand classical buildings by Michelangelo from 1546. The Palace of the Senators (right) is the seat of the city's government.

THE ARCHITECT

In the Renaissance the architect emerged as a separate professional in the building industry. Up until the 15th century men called master masons had designed buildings, managed the building site, and organized the many different workers involved in the construction process. They were men who had trained for many years to acquire the practical skills involved in building. In the Renaissance the jobs of design and construction were separated—architects designed buildings, while contractors, usually masons, handled the practical construction and running of the building site. This change reflected the increased emphasis on theory in the Renaissance—Alberti, for example, was a scholar—and also on artistic creativity. Many Renaissance architects were also artists, the most famous being Raphael and Michelangelo.

rebuilding of Saint Peter's, as well as new roads, bridges, houses, palaces, and squares, and improvements to the city's water supply by restoring old aqueducts and building new ones.

THE CLASSICAL STYLE ABROAD

At first the classical style of building spread abroad only slowly. There were several reasons for this. The style was essentially Italian, and so it seemed foreign in other parts of Europe. At a time when other countries were eager to develop their own identities, they turned to their own traditions of architecture. Another reason for the slow spread of the classical style was its association with the Catholic church, which made it unpopular with Protestant countries.

Nevertheless, the classical style did move gradually beyond Italy. Just as Italian rulers, princes, and popes associated it with the expression of learning and power, so foreign kings came to do the same. These powerful men were the most important patrons. King Henry VIII of England invited

Italian architects to his court, and two English palaces—Nonsuch and Hampton Court—incorporated classical features. In Spain the emperor Charles V commissioned a classical palace in Granada (1526), and his successor Philip II took the idea further in the Escorial (begun 1562), a huge palace and monastery complex near Madrid.

HOW IDEAS SPREAD

Knowledge of the new style was carried by treatises (books) written by Italian architects such as Palladio and Serlio (1475–1554). These treatises were highly illustrated, providing architects with source books of classical features such as columns, moldings, and door and window surrounds, as well as instructions on how to use them.

Ideas were also spread by architects traveling to and from Italy. King Francis I of France (ruled 1515–1547) encouraged Italian artists and architects (including Serlio) to come to his court. Foreign architects could also train or get experience in Italy. The French architect Philibert Delorme (about 1510–1570) studied in Rome for three years before designing many classical buildings in France—including part of the Louvre, the royal palace in Paris—and writing his own treatise on architecture in 1561.

INIGO JONES

The English architect Inigo Jones (1573–1652) visited Italy twice, where he was greatly influenced by Palladio's work. He wrote a treatise on architecture and did more than any other architect to bring a precise interpretation of Italian Renaissance architecture to England. As the classical style took hold throughout Europe, it was taken to colonies in the newly discovered Americas.

Arms and Armor

The Renaissance period saw a dramatic change in arms and warfare. The introduction of missile weapons powered by gunpowder was to transform siege warfare, while on the battlefield heavy cavalry lost its dominant place to foot soldiers armed with pikes, bows, and firearms.

The later Middle Ages, from about 1340 onward, had seen a gradual transition in warfare. The dominance of mounted knights was successfully challenged by various kinds of infantry, the most important being Swiss

Above: **The Battle of San Romano,** *painted by Paolo Uccello about 1450. The cavalry, led by a condottiere riding a white horse, wears chain mail and leather armor and carries lances, swords, and battleaxes.*

pikemen and English longbowmen. The development of gunpowder weapons then further undermined the position of two key elements in medieval warfare—the castle and the mounted knight.

During the period from 1400 to 1650 there were steady developments in warfare technology as firearms assumed greater importance at the expense of more traditional weapons such as pikes, swords, and bows. As protection against firearms, cavalry forces at first adopted heavier armor. Later, however, the trend was for armor

to get lighter to make movement easier. But in 15th-century Italy mercenaries known as condottieri wore increasingly heavy armor to avoid injury in battles that were almost stage-managed.

EARLY FIREARMS

Gunpowder began to be used to propel missiles early in the 14th century. A device resembling a cannon, but intended to shoot arrows, was shown in a manuscript of 1316. By the end of the 14th century firearms were starting to be used all over Europe.

The most important use of firearms to begin with was in siege warfare. In the late medieval period stone-throwing weapons such as the trebuchet were used by attackers in sieges to break down the outer walls of a town or castle they had surrounded and were trying to take. The trebuchet

was a kind of gigantic sling, which was capable of throwing an enormous stone a great distance to batter a hole in a town or castle wall.

These weapons were now replaced by cannons. At the siege of Constantinople by the Turks in 1435 an alarming battery of cannons bombarded the city walls for seven weeks.

Above: Soldiers using cannons to bombard a castle in the early 16th century.

SWISS PIKEMEN

The Swiss infantry had their own special tactics, which made effective use of the pike. The pike was a long, straight piece of wood measuring about 10 ft (3m), tipped with a sharp point of iron. The pikemen formed a square of up to 6,000 men. The outer ranks pointed their pikes at charging cavalry. Any horsemen not toppled by this pike wall would be hacked to death by pikemen inside the square.

The weapons included two enormous guns, each of which could fire a stone ball that weighed over 800 lb. (360kg) and measured 3 ft (1m) across. However, it took two hours to load these mighty guns, and so they could only be fired six or seven times a day.

Early cannons made of cast iron had some serious disadvantages. They were very expensive, and because of impurities in the ore they tended to break apart when fired, killing the gunners. Cannons made of bronze were safer, but even more costly. This problem was not solved until the 16th century, when it was discovered that iron ore from Sweden could be cast into guns that did not explode at the wrong moment.

By the early 16th century cannons were being used in land battles, as the techniques for them loading improved. Moreover, gunners discovered that by placing batteries of cannons at the proper angle, they could be extremely lethal against the massed charge of heavy cavalry or the highly disciplined Swiss infantry.

THE ARQUEBUS AND MUSKET

Hand firearms came into use at the beginning of the 15th century. The early ones were like small versions of a cannon attached to a pike handle. They were followed by the arquebus, which was used by pikemen. The arquebus could only fire a single shot, after which it needed lengthy reloading. During this time the pikeman was vulnerable and needed his pike to protect him while he reloaded. In the early 16th century the Spanish produced a better version of the arquebus—the musket.

The musket was about 6 ft (2m) long and consisted of an iron barrel with a wooden handle. It used lead

Above: A suit of armor from the early 16th century. It was made by riveting metal plates together and was very heavy.

bullets and had a range of about 600 ft (180m). It was used by the Spanish against the French to tremendous effect at the Battle of Pavia in 1525. The Spanish had 17,000 foot soldiers armed with pike and musket. Although the French forces were superior in numbers, they were completely routed by the Spanish musketeers.

As handheld firearms improved and could be reloaded more quickly, the importance of the pike declined. Eventually, at the end of the 17th century the bayonet was invented—attached to the end of a gun, it replaced the pike.

SUITS OF ARMOR

For protection against guns cavalry needed better armor. In medieval warfare heavy cavalry had worn chain mail over hard leather and soft padding, which offered adequate protection without restricting movement too much. Now this was replaced by plate armor, which consisted of metal plates riveted together and covering the whole body. It was very expensive and made movement fairly difficult. Nor did it offer much real protection. If the cavalryman fell from his horse, he could be immobilized like a tortoise on its back and was easily killed.

By the second half of the 16th century it had become clear that wearing too much armor in battle was actually dangerous because it was so heavy it was difficult to move in. Complete body armor began to disappear, and soldiers protected themselves with just helmets and breastplates, which guarded them against fatal head, chest, and abdominal wounds.

SEE ALSO

♦ Chivalry
♦ Condottieri
♦ Fortifications
♦ Warfare

Artists' Workshops

Unlike today, when artists usually work alone, in the Renaissance many people were involved in the production of a single work of art. Painters and sculptors trained and worked in workshops, which were often busy commercial enterprises. A master—an artist who had completed his training—headed the workshop and was helped by apprentices, whom it was his job to teach, and assistants.

In the Middle Ages and the early Renaissance there was little distinction between "art" and "craft." Painters and sculptors were regarded as skillful craftsmen and were expected to achieve high standards of workmanship. Even in the 16th century, when people began to think of artists as intellectuals who created with their minds as well as their hands, a thorough basic training in techniques and materials was still considered essential.

ARTISTS' GUILDS
In Italy and many other parts of Europe artists' workshops were regulated by trade organizations called guilds. Guilds protected the interests of their members by insisting on high standards and preventing outside competition. Young artists were not allowed to sell their work until they had qualified as guild members by completing their apprenticeships.

There is little first-hand information about how artists' workshops were organized in the Renaissance, since few artists left written descriptions. The insights scholars have are gleaned from surviving apprenticeship contracts, financial records, and pictures showing artists at work. A treatise (book) written by the Florentine painter Cennino Cennini (born about 1370) entitled *The Craftsman's Handbook* also contains some general information about how workshops operated.

Apprentices usually entered artists' workshops when they were between 10

Below: A 16th-century illustration showing a typical Renaissance workshop, with an artist sitting at an easel painting a picture.

and 13 years old, although there are many examples of training beginning earlier or later than this. Most apprentices came from fairly lowly social backgrounds or were the sons of

---

A thorough training in materials and techniques was considered essential

---

artists. Workshops were often family affairs and were passed down from father to son. The Bellini family workshop in Venice is one of the best-known examples. Most apprentices were boys. Although a few enterprising women managed to make careers as artists, they were usually trained by tutors at home.

There was no set period for an apprenticeship to last, but Cennini's treatise recommends a minimum of six years, and that was probably about average. So most artists completed their training between the ages of 16 and 20.

There were many tasks involved in creating paintings and sculptures in

Above: An early 15th-century model book from Germany, containing 56 drawings mounted on wooden panels. Books such as this provided artists with a reference source for all the imagery they were likely to need.

Renaissance workshops because, unlike today, artists' materials were not available ready-made. Some of the apprentice's first jobs were to grind pigments (colors), mix paints, and prepare wooden panels with smooth layers of gesso (a hard plasterlike material) ready to be painted on.

Apprentices also practiced drawing. In the early Renaissance this involved copying drawings from books known as pattern or model books. However, it soon also came to include drawing from pieces of sculpture and life models (people).

GREATER RESPONSIBILITIES

Gradually, the apprentice would be allowed to take a share in painting pictures. Initially, he would be entrusted only with minor parts of the design, such as decorative borders, and even trained artists often specialized in painting only a particular part of the picture, such as landscapes or clothes. As the apprentice's skill increased, he would be allowed to paint more until he was capable of producing complete works in his master's style. At the end of his apprenticeship the newly qualified artist usually either continued

---

CATHEDRAL WORKSHOPS

Although most workshops in the Renaissance were run by artists as businesses, there was another sort of workshop. It was a workshop attached to a major architectural project that often took many years to complete, such as a cathedral. It consisted of sheds and drawing offices on the building site. It accommodated all the artists and craftsmen involved in constructing and decorating the building, from architects and masons (builders) to painters and sculptors. Milan cathedral in Italy (begun in 1385) had a thriving workshop that trained masons and stone-carvers to work on the cathedral.

Above: A drawing by the 16th-century Italian artist Parmigiano of a painter's assistant grinding pigments.

to help on all of these projects. Sculptors required more assistants than painters because more tasks were involved in carving and casting a sculpture than creating a painting.

For major commissions a legal contract was drawn up between the artist and the client. It dealt with such matters as the subject of the picture and its size, the quality of materials to be used, the time when it was supposed to be completed, and the price.

Many workshops probably also kept a stock of ready-made designs. Some of Sandro Botticelli's (1445–1510) pictures of the Madonna and Child (Mary and the infant Jesus), for example, exist in several similar versions that were probably produced by his assistants to be bought by customers who could not afford a specially commissioned painting.

INSIDE THE WORKSHOP

We do not know what Botticelli's workshop looked like, but it may have been possible for customers to walk in to it from the street and look at the goods. Several illustrations of the time depict artists at work in rooms that were open to the street when wooden shutters were raised.

Painters' workshops would have been stocked with pigments, slabs to grind them on, sheets of gold leaf for applying to paintings, prepared panels, palettes, and paintbrushes. Sculptors required tools such as saws, hammers, and chisels, and their workshops were bigger because they had to house bulky materials such as clay, bronze, wood, and stone. Workshops would have had pattern books, sketchbooks, prints, and pieces of sculpture for artists to refer to and copy, and would have been furnished with easels, cupboards, stools, and chairs.

to work as an assistant in his master's workshop or became a journeyman—someone who was hired by different masters, usually by the day.

The number of apprentices or assistants in a workshop varied a good deal. Successful artists attracted many pupils, and busy workshops took on extra staff if they had particularly big or specialized commissions to fulfill. Sometimes they also collaborated with other workshops.

RANGE OF PRODUCTS

Most workshops produced a variety of work, including furniture and banners, costumes, and scenery for processions and celebrations, as well as paintings and sculptures. Assistants were needed

Astrology

In the Renaissance many people believed that by studying the sun, moon, planets, and stars, they could predict the future. This study was known as astrology. Astrologers believed that the relative positions of these heavenly bodies had an effect on practically every aspect of life on earth. Today such beliefs are seen as superstition. During the Renaissance, however, people regarded astrology as a science.

Astrology was practiced in many ancient cultures, including ancient Greece, where scholars such as Ptolemy (second century A.D.) wrote extensively on the subject. Their texts were largely forgotten in western Europe during the Middle Ages, and interest in astrology waned until the 12th century, when western scholars began to rediscover Greek texts in Islamic translation. Interest in the subject increased in the 15th and 16th centuries, when scholars studied ancient Greek texts afresh.

The Renaissance view of the universe was based on Ptolemy. People

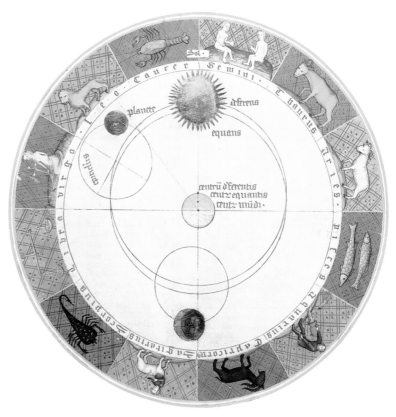

Above: This astrological chart shows the earth, sun, and planets encircled by the zodiac belt, divided into 12 different signs. Astrologers used charts such as this to predict the future.

thought that the earth was at the center of the universe and that seven planets—the sun, the moon, Mercury, Venus, Mars, Saturn, and Jupiter—rotated around it. Beyond them at the outer edge of the universe other stars revolved inside a large crystal sphere.

Astrologers devised often complex systems and procedures in order to apply the movements of the planets to earthly events. Most importantly, they

THE PROBLEM OF FATE AND FREE WILL

Astrology posed philosophical problems regarding people's fate and free will. If the stars can tell the future, and a person's fate is already determined, then free will is an illusion, and people do not bear responsibility for their actions. Philosophers generally argued either that the soul was divine and not subject to the influences of the stars, or that astrology merely interpreted divine will and that people's responsibility was to conform to the predictions. The Italian philosopher and theologian Marsilio Ficino (1433–1499) believed that people's souls were a divine link with God and that they were influenced by the planets, but he also believed that people could use the influences if they understood them.

imagined the course of the sun around the earth as a circle and divided this circle into 12 equal parts. They called each part a house and ascribed a sign to it. They were known as signs of the zodiac and were named after constellations of stars. Among them were Aries (the ram), Aquarius (the water

Astrologers thought that each planet, star, and sign of the zodiac corresponded to various properties

carrier), and Sagittarius (the archer). Astrologers thought that each planet, star, and sign of the zodiac corresponded to various properties and influences. They had to learn to interpret these signs depending on the relative positions of heavenly bodies in the sky, and they used books, charts, tables, globes, and models of the heavens to help them.

THE ROLE OF ASTROLOGY

Astrology was an important part of people's lives, and astrologers were consulted for all manner of advice. They were employed by rulers to help calculate the best time to undertake activities such as coronations or battles and even to advise on the best clothes to wear for certain occasions. Queen Elizabeth I of England employed the famous astrologer, alchemist, and mathematician John Dee (1527–1608) as her court astrologer.

Astrologers were also consulted on the best time to practice medicine; indeed, many physicians were also astrologers. Plants (from which most medicines were made) and different parts of the body were associated with signs of the zodiac, and so the position of the planets was thought to affect the healing powers of medicines.

Astrologers were also called on to determine an individual's life or character according to their date of birth, to find answers to specific questions, or to reveal the future of human affairs. This last activity, also known as judicial astrology, was often discounted by natural philosophers (early scientists), even though they believed in the influence of heavenly bodies. Indeed, by 1600 many aspects of astrology were discredited as advances were made in astronomy, the objective study of the universe.

Above: This 16th-century woodcut shows two astrologers examining the positions of the stars.

SEE ALSO

♦ Astronomy
♦ Magic and Superstition
♦ Medicine and Surgery
♦ Neoplatonism

Astronomy

In the Middle Ages people believed that the earth was the center of the universe. Later astronomers, however, started to question this idea and to suggest that the sun was at the center. This completely changed people's view of their place in the universe—and also laid the foundations for modern astronomy.

At the beginning of the 15th century people's ideas as to how the heavenly bodies were arranged in the sky had not changed for over 1,500 years. Since the time of the ancient Greeks astronomers had believed that the earth was the center of the universe, and the sun, planets, and stars revolved around it. These ideas were written down in the second century of our era by the Greek astronomer Claudius Ptolemy.

However, this geocentric (earth-centered) theory did not explain several things that astronomers had noticed in their observations of the planets. One was that the planets

Above: Tycho Brahe's observatory, built on an island off the coast of Denmark. It was here that Brahe was able to observe the appearance of a new star in 1572 and follow the path of a comet in 1577.

THE PTOLEMAIC SYSTEM

Claudius Ptolemy was a Greek astronomer who lived in Alexandria, Egypt, from about 100 to 170 A.D. He wrote a great book on astronomy, known as *The Almagest*, which included the ideas of the Greek philosopher Aristotle, plus his own observations and those of other Greek astronomers.

In Ptolemy's system the earth was stationary at the center of the planetary system, while the sun, moon, and planets—Mercury, Venus, Mars, Jupiter, and Saturn—spun around it in perfect circles, each one carried on a transparent celestial crystal sphere. All the other stars were attached to a great sphere that enclosed the whole system. Because these outer stars did not appear to move in relation to each other, they were called the "fixed stars." The whole heavens moved around the earth, creating day and night.

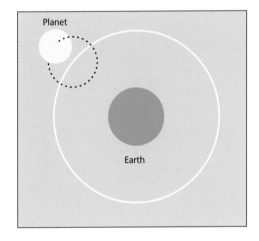

Left: A diagram of an epicycle, a small circle spinning around a larger one.

Below: Ptolemy's view of the universe. The sun, moon, and planets circle the earth at the center.

The German astronomer Johann Regiomontanus (1436–1476) drew on his own observations of the stars and planets in order to correct Ptolemy's star tables (a star table is a catalog of stars that enables an astronomer to determine the location of any star or planet on any given day). After Regiomontanus died, other astronomers continued this work for 40 years, producing a much more accurate set of star tables.

appeared to move nearer and farther away from the earth in the course of their orbits. Another was that unlike a star, which appears to travel directly across the heavens, a planet (which means "wanderer") appears to back up for a time, then go forward again. The planets go through dozens of such cycles in the course of making their way across the sky.

TURNING IN SMALL CIRCLES

Ptolemy himself had devised one explanation for the irregular motion of the planets. He said that instead of going around the earth in a perfect circle, each planet turned in a small circle of its own, which rotated around the larger circle. These small circles were called epicycles.

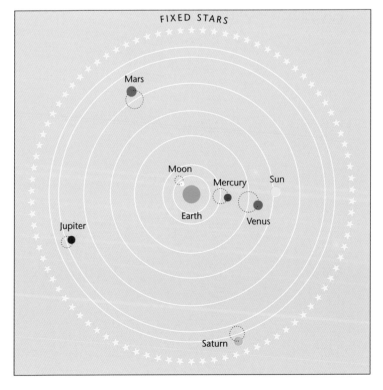

This improved set of star tables made a major contribution to the work of the Polish astronomer Nicolaus Copernicus (1473–1543). As a young man Copernicus studied in Italy in the late 15th century, at a time when the church was calling for an improved calendar. The idea of reforming the calendar captured Copernicus's imagination, but he realized it was not yet possible to do this, because astronomical knowledge was not good enough to correct the calendar.

THE SUN AT THE CENTER

Copernicus decided that Ptolemy's explanation of the motions of the planets was too complicated to be right. Instead, Copernicus devised a different system. He placed the sun in the center of the universe, with the earth, planets, and stars revolving around it. This system accounted for most of the apparent motions of the heavenly bodies. It did not explain them all because Copernicus still

Below: Copernicus's view of the universe places the sun at the center. The earth and planets spin around it, moving in epicycles around their circular paths. On the outer sphere are the fixed stars, which do not appear to move.

believed the earth's path around the sun was circular (it is actually an ellipse—a flattened circle). Copernicus also proposed that the earth spun around on its axis once every day, which would explain why the stars in the sky appeared to revolve around it.

About 30 years after concluding that the sun was the center of the universe, Copernicus explained his revolutionary heliocentric (sun-centered) theory in his book *The Revolutions of the Heavenly Spheres* (1543). After the book's publication knowledge of his theory spread across Europe, but very few astronomers were convinced by it.

TYCHO BRAHE

In 1572 the appearance of a new star, a nova, astounded astronomers. This first nova ever to be recorded in Europe was observed by the Danish astronomer Tycho Brahe. Brahe had been given an island by the Danish king for the purpose of building a large observatory. There he made many remarkable observations of the heavens, and he was able to determine that the nova was among the "fixed stars," where traditional astronomy had maintained no change could take place. Five years later a huge comet blazed across the heavens, and Brahe again determined that it was beyond the moon, not close to earth, as traditional astronomy insisted it should be.

Brahe did not accept the heliocentric theory, however. He felt the arguments against the earth moving were too strong. Instead, he suggested the earth was at the center, while the sun and moon circled the earth, and the planets circled the sun. This theory solved some of the problems in Ptolemy's system, while avoiding the issue of how a huge body like the earth could stay in motion around the sun.

FIXED STARS

Saturn

Venus

Earth

Sun

Moon

Jupiter

Mercury

Mars

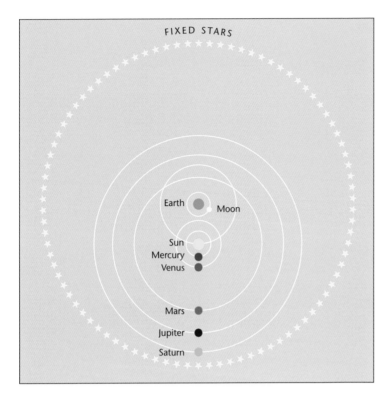

FIXED STARS

Earth Moon

Sun
Mercury
Venus

Mars

Jupiter

Saturn

Above: Tycho Brahe's view of the planetary system. Here the earth is at the center again, circled by the sun and the moon. The planets, however, circle the sun.

SEE ALSO

♦ Astrology
♦ Copernicus
♦ Galileo

Brahe's student, Johannes Kepler (1571–1630), inherited his tables of observations. He was influenced by the ancient Greek mathematician Pythagoras, who believed that the universe was made up of numbers and geometric shapes. Following this idea, Kepler tried to fit Brahe's tables of planetary motions into geometric shapes. After many years of observations he found that the paths of the planets formed the shape of ellipses. Once the idea of an elliptical path for a planet was accepted, there was no longer any need for the Ptolemaic epicycles. In his books *The New Astronomy* (1609) and *Harmony of the Universe* (1619) Kepler explained the laws of planetary motions in a sun-centered system.

GALILEO
The Italian astronomer Galileo Galilei (1564–1642) heard about the newly invented telescope in 1609. He set about constructing his own telescope, refining it and transforming it into an instrument suitable for astronomical observation. Among the sights it revealed were the craters of the moon, thousands of new stars, four moons of Jupiter, and sunspots.

Galileo published several books in which he announced his discoveries and proclaimed that they proved that Copernicus's ideas had been right. But early in the 17th century the Catholic church had become hostile to the idea that the sun was the center of the universe. This was partly because of the radical theories of Giordano Bruno, who had been executed for heresy in 1600 for declaring that there was an infinite number of worlds all inhabited by human beings.

PLACED UNDER HOUSE ARREST
In 1616 the church ordered Galileo to stop teaching the theory of heliocentrism, and he refrained from publishing anything more until his *Dialogue of the Two World Systems* appeared in 1632. In 1633 he was found guilty of violating the church's order and was placed under house arrest for the rest of his life.

This did not stop Galileo's inquiring mind—he now turned his attention to the problem of motion. The traditional explanation for motion was that objects fell to the earth because they were returning to their natural resting place in the center of the universe. This idea was badly undermined by placing the sun in the center of the planetary system—and how could the earth spin around the sun? Galileo came up with his theory of inertia, which said that a body set in motion will remain in motion until stopped by an external force. This provided an explanation of how the earth could stay in motion around the sun—which was the culminating point of Renaissance astronomy.

Bankers and Banking

Banking is the business of dealing in money—holding it, lending it, and exchanging it for different currencies. Some of the earliest bankers were merchants. As well as trading in goods, merchants became involved in lending money and transferring funds from one place to another. As they became more involved with money transactions, they became merchant-bankers.

Trading in distant lands was a risky business in the late Middle Ages, so merchants often formed partnerships to undertake trading enterprises. Partnerships were simple arrangements at first. The partners agreed to raise the investment capital jointly, to divide the profits (or losses) from the enterprise, and to share the physical dangers of traveling abroad. However, partnerships had a serious drawback. Each partner was responsible for the whole debt if the partnership lost money.

LIMITED LOSSES

As time went by, partnerships were replaced by the *commenda* agreement. Under the terms of this agreement one merchant (the capitalist) would provide the funds for several traveling merchants, who were generally much younger men. The advantage of the *commenda* agreement was that losses were limited to the amount invested.

Below: A 14th-century bank shown in a manuscript of that time.

DOUBLE-ENTRY BOOKKEEPING

Double-entry bookkeeping was a special way of keeping accounts that developed in Italy around 1300. It involved making two entries in an accounting ledger for every financial transaction. When an item of goods was bought or sold, the transaction would be entered as a debit entry against the merchant who sold the goods (because he no longer had the goods and was owed money for them) and as a credit entry against the merchant who bought the goods (because he now had the goods and had not yet paid for them). When the buyer paid the money due, this was entered as a debit item against the buyer and as a credit item against the seller. This new accounting technique helped merchants and bankers keep track of the increasing number of financial transactions.

Right: An accounting ledger from the Medici banking house in Florence. Bankers had to keep very careful records of every transaction, entering the details twice over, as both a credit and a debit.

Later still it became the practice for the men who went abroad to remain there for several years, acting as agents for the merchant-capitalists back home. These agents were called factors; and rather than traveling with the goods they bought abroad, they organized shipments of goods back to their homeland or to another place where they could be sold. When the agreement ended, the factor returned home, where profits and losses were tallied up and divided according to the terms of the agreement.

Merchant-bankers made use of *commenda* agreements to create far-flung networks for their commercial and financial activities By 1300 the powerful banking families of Bardi and Peruzzi were established in Florence, with their factors operating branches all over Europe and in some parts of the Middle East. Although these banking houses collapsed in the 1340s, by the 1470s the city had more than 30 banking houses, including the great bank of the Medici.

The Medici bank was more centralized than the Bardi and Peruzzi firms had been, and Cosimo de Medici exercised a greater degree of control over his factors than his predecessors had. Nevertheless, the Medici were unable to avoid the pitfall that threatened all financial institutions at that time—making bad loans to powerful princes.

TRANSFERRING FUNDS

The rapid increase in trade made it essential for bankers to find a more efficient way of transferring funds from one place to another. Up until this time goods had been exchanged either for

Left: Merchants transacting business in a bank in Florence in the late 15th century.

other goods or for coins made of some precious metal—gold or silver (bullion). Now the stock of bullion was too small to support the volume of trade.

GIRO BANKING

To overcome this problem, the banks devised ways of facilitating trade deals that did not involve bullion. One was a system of giro banking for paying bills. A merchant who had bought goods could instruct his bank to transfer credit for the amount involved to the account of the merchant who had sold the goods. This kind of paper transaction involved the use of double-entry bookkeeping.

Banks made money in various ways. They took deposits from some clients and loaned money to others at a higher rate of interest. They also exchanged one currency for another—which

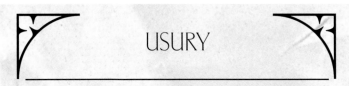

USURY

In the Renaissance period the term usury meant lending money in return for a fixed rate of interest. The practice was condemned by the church as avarice, one of the seven deadly sins, for which perpetrators would suffer eternal damnation. Nevertheless, people needed to borrow money. Some people resorted to Jewish money-lenders, who were not affected by the church's disapproval. Others borrowed money from merchant-bankers, who often charged more than 30 percent per year on the loans they made.

In the early 16th century, however, Johann Eck, a German university professor, came up with an ingenious solution to the problem. He devised a system of three related contracts, which turned what was essentially interest on a loan into a profit on a commercial transaction. This satisfied the church authorities and enabled bankers to make loans without being accused of usury. Bankers could also claim that their gains were profits made on currency exchanges. The account books of the Medici bank, for instance, contain no entries for interest income, but entries for "profit and loss on Exchange."

helped traveling merchants, who could exchange their own currency for the local one wherever they were. Banks made money on the deal by taking advantage of different exchange rates.

BILL OF EXCHANGE

Another facility offered by banks was the bill of exchange, which was a contract in which a borrower promised to repay his loan on a specified date and in a different currency. A merchant in Venice might borrow 1,000 ducats (the Venetian currency) from a Venetian bank. He would sign a bill of exchange agreeing to repay the sum 90 days later in English shillings at the London office of the same bank at the Venetian rate of exchange. On the day the bill was due to be paid, the merchant would visit the London branch and pay the specified amount. In Venice, however, a ducat could buy more shillings than it could in London. So when the merchant repaid his loan in London at the Venetian rate, he handed over more shillings than his ducats were worth in London. So the bank made a profit.

Italian banks dominated European finance during the early Renaissance period. However, by the end of the 15th century banks were appearing in other parts of Europe as well. Banking houses in the southern German cities of Augsburg and Nuremberg were particularly successful. That was because these cities were well placed on some of the main European trade routes, and they had factors in Venice who arranged for the transport of goods from the Mediterranean region into central Europe.

GERMAN BANKERS

Because these cities were flourishing trading centers, several family firms of merchant-bankers rose to prominence there, including the Welsers, the Hochstetters, the Paumgartners, and the Fuggers. These southern German bankers made money not only through normal banking processes, but also from the mining of silver and other ores. Augsburg and Nuremberg were geographically close to sources of metallic ores in the eastern Alps and on

Right: The marketplace in Augsburg. Augsburg was one of two prosperous southern German cities (the other was Nuremberg) where bankers flourished during the 15th and 16th centuries.

JAKOB FUGGER

Jakob Fugger was born in Augsburg in 1459, the son of a modestly wealthy family. His ancestor Johannes Fugger had been a master weaver who had settled in Augsburg in 1368, and his sons had become merchants dealing in silks, spices, and woolen cloth from Venice. Jakob spent his early years as an apprentice in Venice, where he learned the subtle arts of double-entry book-keeping and other Italian financial skills.

Jakob returned home to Augsburg to become a merchant at the age of 19. He was soon expanding his activities from the Venetian trade into financial ventures. His first major business deal came in the 1480s, when he

began making loans to members of the powerful Hapsburg family. In return he gained rights to copper and silver mines in Hungary and the Tyrol. Jakob Fugger had no children; and following the deaths of his brothers, he made his nephews partners in the firm. However, he remained in control of his banking empire until his death in 1525, saying that he intended to continue making money as long as he could.

Left: Jakob Fugger at work in his banking house in Augsburg. As banker to the powerful Hapsburg family, Fugger became the most successful banker in Europe.

the fringes of Bohemia and Hungary. Mining had gone on in these districts for centuries, and the surface veins were almost exhausted. But in the 15th century new techniques allowed miners to sink shafts deep into the bowels of the earth and also to squeeze more metal out of the ores that were dug up.

THE RICHEST BANKER OF ALL

Some of the richest mining districts lay on lands belonging to the Hapsburg dynasty, which was one of the most powerful families in Europe. Southern German bankers financed the Hapsburgs' ambitious political schemes in return for concessions that allowed them to exploit these advances in mining and metalworking.

The banker who profited most from this kind of arrangement was Jakob Fugger. In the 1480s he made a series of loans to the Hapsburg duke Sigmund, who gave him major concessions in silver and copper mining in the Tyrol region. Later loans made to the Hapsburg emperors Maximilian I and Charles V brought more mineral concessions in the Tyrol and Hungary, which were to make Fugger the richest banker in Europe. Ironically, it was the close relationship Fugger had with the Hapsburgs that eventually brought the Fugger banking house down. Loans that were made to finance the excessive ambitions of Charles' son, Philip II of Spain, were never repaid, and after 1576 the Fugger fortunes declined.

SEE ALSO
♦ Capitalism
♦ Merchants
♦ Trade
♦ Wealth

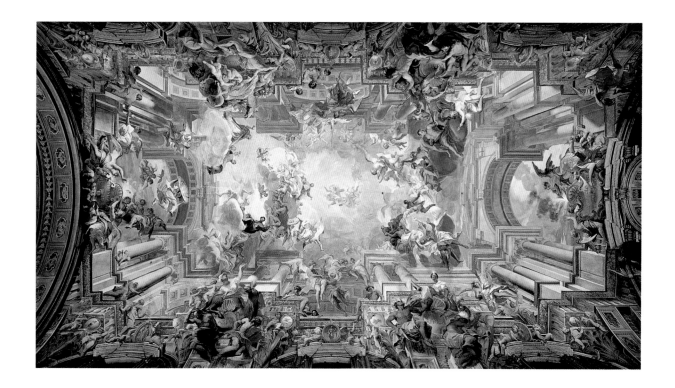

Baroque

The term "baroque" is used to describe the style that dominated painting, sculpture, and architecture in the 17th and 18th centuries in Europe. The baroque style is characterized by its large scale, grandness, and powerful sense of drama and movement.

Baroque art was closely linked with the religious movement known as the Counter Reformation, in which the Roman Catholic church sought to renew itself and to assert itself against the Protestant groups that had broken away in the early 16th century. Many of the Catholic church's ideas for strengthening itself were formulated at the Council of Trent (1545–1563).

The role of art in religion was one of the subjects discussed by the council. It declared that artists should work in a realistic style to inspire the faithful "to adore and love God and cultivate piety."

This statement stimulated some artists to move away from another style known as mannerism, which was popular in Florence and Rome in the middle of the 16th century. Mannerist artists such as Bronzino produced highly refined works of art in which they exaggerated appearances to make the figures and objects they portrayed look more elegant. Their work reflected the sophisticated tastes of princely patrons such as the Medici for whom it was produced. Baroque painters and sculptors reacted to this "mannered"

Above: This painting by the 17th-century painter Andrea Pozzo decorates the ceiling of the church of Sant' Ignazio in Rome. It shows the Entry of Saint Ignatius into Heaven and displays the drama and movement characteristic of the baroque style.

style and began to emphasize more weighty and lifelike figures in their work. In keeping with the church's teaching, they tried to create work that would have a strong emotional effect on the people who looked at it, to make them feel personally involved in the spiritual agonies and ecstasies of the saints and holy figures portrayed.

ANNIBALE CARRACCI

Two Italian painters, Annibale Carracci (1560–1609) and Michelangelo da Caravaggio (1573–1610), were very important in the creation of the baroque style. Carracci admired the simplicity and beauty of Raphael's work, which he sought to reflect in his own paintings.

His picture *The Virgin Mourning Christ* (about 1600) shows Raphael's influence in the idealized beauty of Mary's face, the smooth, pale body of Christ and the simple composition (arrangement), in which the grieving figure of Mary and the dead body of Christ form a triangle. However, the powerful emotion expressed in Mary's face and the dramatic use of light and shade to emphasize Christ's body are typical of the baroque style.

MICHELANGELO DA CARAVAGGIO

In some ways Caravaggio's paintings are very different from Carracci's. The figures are not painted in an idealized way, but are strikingly realistic. Caravaggio often used people he met in the streets as his models and made no attempt to beautify them—they are often grubby and with ragged clothes.

The Crucifixion of Saint Peter (1600–1601) is typical of Caravaggio's religious paintings. The way he painted the man on the left-hand side, as if his bottom and dirty feet are sticking out of the picture, shocked many people.

However, along with its realism the painting is characterized by its weighty figures, its powerful sense of movement as the men heave and pull Saint Peter's cross, and its dramatic use of light and shade. It is these qualities that make the picture baroque.

ILLUSIONIST CEILINGS

Caravaggio and Carracci produced many paintings that were not for churches. Carracci's most famous work is a ceiling painted with scenes from classical myth in the Farnese Palace in Rome (1597). Large-scale decorative schemes such as this were influenced by Michelangelo's ceiling in the Sistine Chapel (1508–1512) and were some of the most outstanding achievements of

Above: **The Crucifixion of Saint Peter** *(1600–1601), one of three paintings by Caravaggio in the church of Santa Maria del Popolo in Rome. Its dramatic lighting and strong composition are typically baroque.*

GIANLORENZO BERNINI

Gianlorenzo Bernini (1598–1680) was the most outstanding artist of his generation in Rome. He transformed the appearance of the city with his buildings, statues, and fountains executed for powerful patrons, including the Borghese family and several popes. He was a remarkably skilled sculptor who could carve marble with great delicacy to appear like human skin and with great drama to create cascading folds of drapery (clothing). These qualities are perfectly shown in his sculpture *The Ecstasy of Saint Theresa* (1645–1652). It shows a vision described by Saint Theresa in which an angel pierced her heart with an arrow. She was filled with pain but also bliss, and Bernini shows her floating up to heaven, with golden rays of light pouring down behind her.

Right: Bernini's sculpture The Ecstasy of Saint Theresa *(1645–1652) in the Cornaro Chapel in the Church of Santa Maria della Vittoria in Rome.*

baroque painters. Such decorative schemes include the ceilings in the Barbarini Palace (begun about 1633) in Rome and the Palazzo Pitti (1637–1639) in Florence, both by Pietro da Cortona (1596–1669), and the ceiling in the church of San Ignazio (1691–1694) by Andrea Pozzo (1642–1709).

All these ceilings are illusionistic or trompe l'oeil (a French term which means "to trick the eye"). They are painted to create the illusion that there is no roof and that the building opens directly to the sky. Against the background of the sky the painted ceilings are packed full of figures.

ARCHITECTURE AND SCULPTURE
The baroque style was taken up by sculptors and architects as well as painters. Gianlorenzo Bernini (see box), the most influential baroque artist working in Rome in the first half

of the 17th century, excelled in all three art forms. His major rival in architecture was Francesco Borromini (1599–1667), who also worked in the baroque style.

Their approach is illustrated by two projects: the sweeping colonnades (begun 1656) that Bernini built around the square in front of Saint Peter's in Rome and Borromini's Church of Santa Agnese (1653), also in Rome. Both use classical features derived from Renaissance architecture, such as columns, domes, and round arches, combined with a dynamic sense of movement. The sweep of Bernini's colonnade draws people toward Saint Peter's. Like Borromini's curvaceous, sculptural design for Santa Agnese, its effect is dramatic and theatrical.

In the 17th century Rome attracted artists from many countries who came to learn from the city's ancient and

Renaissance art, as well as from the work of contemporary artists. When these visiting artists returned home, they helped spread the baroque style throughout Europe. The Flemish painter Peter Paul Rubens (1577–1640) was the most influential of these artists (see box).

Baroque art was popular in Roman Catholic countries like Spain and Portugal, and spread to their colonies in Latin America, such as Mexico. However, it had less impact in countries that had become Protestant. This difference reflected the ways Catholics and Protestants worshiped. Catholics had elaborate rituals, and their churches were richly decorated, while Protestants favored simpler rituals and plainer churches.

ROYAL GLORY

As in Italy, the baroque style was not confined to religious art. In France, for example, King Louis XIV (1643–1715) realized that its visual pomp and splendor could be used to promote the idea of royal glory. His huge palace at Versailles, built mainly in the 1670s, is one of the most spectacular examples of the baroque style. It combines architecture, painting, sculpture, the

PETER PAUL RUBENS

Peter Paul Rubens (1577–1640) was the greatest baroque painter in northern Europe. He lived in Flanders (now part of Belgium) but as a young man spent eight years in Italy, where he was influenced by the work of Carracci and Caravaggio. He took the Italian baroque taste for large paintings full of drama back to Antwerp and was an immediate success. His patrons included powerful rulers such as King Louis XIII of France, King Philip III of Spain, and King Charles I of England. They held him in high regard and often asked him to undertake diplomatic missions for them as well as paintings. Rubens' pictures are characterized by their rich colors, free brushwork, full-figured ladies, and exuberance. He produced an astonishing number of paintings and ran a huge workshop of assistants to enable him to keep up with all his commissions.

decorative arts, and garden design to create an overwhelming testimony to his power and wealth.

The baroque style lasted into the mid-18th century in parts of Europe and Latin America, but in France it gave way to a lighter, more playful style called the rococo in about 1700. Toward the end of the 18th century both the baroque and rococo went out of fashion when artists sought to revive the art of ancient Greece and Rome in a very precise style called neoclassicism.

SEE ALSO

- Architecture
- Artists' Workshops
- Classicism
- Counter Reformation
- Mannerism
- Painting
- Patronage
- Sculpture

Left: The palace of Versailles, designed for King Louis XIV of France by Louis le Vau and Jules Hardouin-Mansart between 1655 and 1682. It is baroque in its huge scale and combination of architecture, sculpture, and garden design.

Bavaria

Bavaria is a large state in the southeast part of Germany. During the Renaissance it was part of the Holy Roman Empire and had been ruled by the dukes of Wittelsbach since the 12th century. However, because when one duke died the duchy was divided up among his sons, rather than passing to the eldest son, by the mid-14th century Bavaria was divided into several rival duchies.

This division of power had some benefits, however. While the dukes feuded, an assembly called the *Landtag* took over control of government and taxes. The towns became wealthy through trade and were largely independent of the dukes. Because of the divisions among the nobility, Bavaria began to develop democratic forms of government and an independent spirit of citizenship.

After 1450 the Wittelsbach dukes began slowly to create a unified principality, and this process was helped when, in 1506, the rule of primogeniture, under which the eldest son inherits, was brought in. Bavaria was finally reunified under the rule of Duke William IV in 1545. Munich became the capital of the reunited duchy—and its position on the main road between Salzburg and Augsburg meant that the dukes were able to charge tolls from travelers and merchants, which helped swell their revenues.

A PRACTICAL PRINCE
Although William was a Catholic and a fierce opponent of the Protestant Reformation, he was also a practical

Above: The monastery of Andechs, which was built in 1455 by Albert III to house sacred relics.

prince who did not allow religion to affect his politics. At first he formed an alliance with the Protestant Schmalkaldic League to protect himself from the power of the Catholic Hapsburgs. But when Protestantism threatened to encroach on his territory, he promptly changed sides. From the mid-16th century, when Duke Albert V came to power, Protestantism was completely outlawed in Bavaria.

LEGENDS OF THE PAST

The Wittelsbachs were clever in using propaganda to increase their prestige. They cultivated legends about Bavaria's past and encouraged pilgrims to come to the duchy. With this in view Duke Albert III built a monastery in 1455 on a promontory southwest of Munich, on the ruins of a castle once owned by the Andechs dynasty. A chapel there housed sacred relics from Jerusalem that had been lost when the Andechs had died out, but now (it was said) were miraculously rediscovered. The pilgrims who came to the "holy mountain" to see these relics helped increase the prestige of the Wittelsbachs and put Bavaria on the map.

The humanist and historian Johannes Aventinus also contributed to the Bavarian sense of identity. He was tutor to Duke William's younger brothers in the early years of the 16th century, and he rummaged through the ducal archives to find the material to write a chronicle of the Bavarian dukes.

MUNICH

During the 15th and 16th centuries Munich became an important city. Much new building was done, including the Frauen Church (begun 1468) and the town hall (begun 1470). In 1538 construction began on the Michalskirche in Munich, one of the largest Renaissance churches in northern Europe. In another bid to boost the prestige of the Wittelsbachs, sculptures on the front of this church hinted at a blood relationship between the Wittelsbachs and Charlemagne, the founder of the Holy Roman Empire.

In the 16th century Munich became a vibrant center of Renaissance culture. Duke Albert V brought to the city the great Flemish musician Orlando di Lasso in 1556, as well as Friedrich Sustris, the Dutch architect, painter, and sculptor.

The Michalskirche was completed in 1597, when Maximilian I, one of the most important Wittelsbachs, was duke. He used his position as a leader of the Catholic League to increase the power of his line. He was so successful that the rule of the Wittelsbachs was to last until the early 20th century.

SEE ALSO

♦ Germany
♦ Holy Roman Empire

Below: An illustration from a 16th-century manuscript showing the Flemish composer Orlando di Lasso directing musicians in the chapel of the Bavarian court.

Bellini, Giovanni

Above: **Madonna of the Meadow,** *painted by Bellini about 1505. It shows Mary and the baby Jesus with fields, a village, and hills beyond.*

Giovanni Bellini (about 1430–1516) was the first Venetian painter to introduce Renaissance ideas into his pictures. He brought a naturalistic, or lifelike, appearance to his paintings and worked in oil paint, a new material that had just been introduced to Italy from northern Europe. He developed a style based on rich, warm colors that came to characterize Venetian painting.

Bellini came from a family of painters. His father Jacopo (about 1400–1470) ran a successful workshop in which Giovanni and his brother Gentile (about 1429–1507) trained. His sister married Andrea Mantegna (1431–1506), an artist whose precise style influenced Bellini's early work. By the 1470s Bellini had become famous. His pictures were sought by Venetian and foreign rulers, and in 1483 he was made painter to the Republic of Venice.

Bellini is best known for his religious pictures, particularly ones representing Mary and the infant Jesus, known as the Madonna and Child. These paintings range from small, tender portrayals intended for private devotion, such as *Madonna of the Meadow* (about 1505), to very large and majestic paintings to go behind altars in churches. His grandest work of this type is *The Madonna and Child Enthroned with Saints* (1505) in the church of San Zaccaria in Venice.

REALISTIC APPEARANCES

Bellini's paintings show his concern for realistic appearances. His figures look weighty, their skin is rendered with great delicacy, and there is a sense of space around them. He often painted landscapes in the background, capturing the way distant hills appear to melt away into a delicate blue haze—an effect that is known as aerial perspective. His observation of nature is most apparent in his meticulous portraits, such as that of Doge Leonardo Loredano (1501).

Bellini was able to achieve subtle effects and rich colors by developing the new technique of oil painting that had just been introduced to Italy from northern Europe. He blended the slow-drying oil paints into each other as he worked and used glazes—thin, almost transparent layers of paint—to build up rich, glowing colors. Bellini's advances in oil painting, his subtle technique, and his use of color were developed by his two most famous pupils, Giorgione (about 1477–1510) and Titian (about 1487–1576).

Biblical Studies

For most of the Middle Ages there was only one official version of the Bible in use in the Catholic church—the Vulgate version, which had been translated into Latin by Saint Jerome in 405. Since only an educated elite could read Latin, most people depended on priests to explain the Scriptures to them.

This situation began to change in the 14th century, when an English scholar began to urge that people should be allowed to read the Bible themselves in their own language. John Wycliffe (about 1330–1384) was heavily critical of the Catholic church, which he saw as corrupt and out of touch. He believed that the only true authority on religious matters was the Bible itself. To allow as many people as possible to read the scriptures, he began to oversee an official English version of the Bible. Wycliffe's ideas challenged those of the Catholic church, and he was branded a heretic (someone whose beliefs contradict those of the church).

THE WORK OF ERASMUS

Catholic scholars and priests also worked on new versions of the Bible. One was Desiderius Erasmus (about 1466–1536), who devoted years to the study and recovery of the original Greek texts of the New Testament. In 1516 he published an edition that contained a new Greek version of the gospels and a more accurate Latin translation of them, which soon took over from the Vulgate as the version in the most widespread use.

In the preface to his edition of the Bible Erasmus made an eloquent plea for more versions of the scriptures to be translated into the vernacular, or common, languages of the people of Europe. Six years after the publication of Erasmus's Greek version of the New Testament the monk Martin Luther (1483–1546) began to translate the scriptures into his native language of German. The translation of the scriptures into local languages became an important aspect of Protestantism, the branch of Christianity that formally broke with the Catholic church in the 16th century.

Above: The Dutch scholar Desiderius Erasmus, who produced new translations of the scriptures.

SEE ALSO

♦ Erasmus
♦ Humanism
♦ Luther
♦ Protestantism
♦ Reformation
♦ Religious Dissent

Boccaccio

Above: This 15th-century painting by the artist Sandro Botticelli illustrates a story from Boccaccio's Decameron *in which a huntsman sets his dogs on a naked woman.*

Giovanni Boccaccio (1313–1375) was an Italian writer who had a great influence on Renaissance literature. His poems and stories, written in his native tongue rather than Latin, were to inspire many later writers, notably Chaucer and Shakespeare.

Boccaccio was the son of a Florentine banker. He studied law and banking in Naples, where he wrote some of his early works. They were allegedly inspired by a woman with whom he fell in love while in Naples. Boccaccio may have written *Il Filocolo* ("Love's Labor"), a prose romance written in Italian, at her request. Another early work in Italian was *Filostrato*, the story of Troilus and Cressida. It was the first narrative poem written in a verse form called *ottava rima* (octave rhyme), in which each verse consisted of eight lines—a form earlier used by minstrels for their songs.

In 1340 Boccaccio returned to Florence, where he wrote *Elegy of Madam Fiammetta*, which is sometimes seen as the first psychological novel, and the *Comedy of Florentine Nymphs*, a pastoral narrative (a story set in an idealized countryside). This type of story became very popular.

In 1350 Boccaccio met the poet Petrarch, who became his friend. The two men developed a passion for classical Greek and Latin literature. Inspired by Petrarch, Boccaccio wrote several works in Latin, including an encyclopedia of classical mythology entitled *Genealogy of the Gods*.

THE DECAMERON

The work that brought Boccaccio the greatest fame, however, was the *Decameron* ("Ten Days"), written in 1353. It consists of 100 short stories supposedly told over 10 days by Florentine youths who had fled plague-ridden Florence. The witty tales that filled the *Decameron* increased the

---

The work that brought Boccaccio the greatest fame was the Decameron

---

popularity of the novella (a short story that often has a surprise or comic ending). Its fresh, original style and use of the vernacular (native language) were to make the *Decameron* a model for prose literature throughout Europe for the next three centuries.

SEE ALSO
♦ Chaucer
♦ Dante
♦ Humanism
♦ Literature
♦ Petrarch
♦ Shakespeare

Bohemia

The central European kingdom of Bohemia lay to the northeast of Bavaria and occupied the region that is now the Czech Republic. It was part of the Holy Roman Empire, and in 1355 its king, Charles I of Bohemia, became the Holy Roman emperor Charles IV. One of Charles' first acts as emperor was to issue an official proclamation called the Golden Bull of 1355, which (among other things) established that the king of Bohemia would from that time be one of the seven people who elected the emperor. This act alone made Bohemia a kingdom to be reckoned with.

Charles did much more to promote his own kingdom. He had already founded the University of Prague in 1348, and now he greatly increased the size and importance of the city, which he made his main residence and capital of the empire. However, tensions were rising at this time between the Slavic Czechs and the Germans who populated the city. Charles encouraged a sense of Slavic identity by promoting legends of a visit to Bohemia by the Greek brothers Cyril and Methodius, who had been missionaries in Slavic central Europe during the ninth century.

TIES WITH ENGLAND

In 1382 Charles arranged the marriage of his 16-year-old daughter, Anne of Bohemia, to King Richard II of England. This opened up cultural exchanges between the two countries. Bohemian students in England became interested in the writings of the English religious reformer John Wycliffe. They smuggled some of his writings back to Prague, where religious dissent began to grow among members of the university. A crisis came in 1415, when the Czech dissident Jan Hus (see box on page 66) was burned at the stake for heresy. A sense of outrage swept through the Czech population. For a time violence

Above: The city of Prague, the capital of Renaissance Bohemia. Prague was built on the banks of the Vltava River, at a point where trade routes linking the north and south of Europe met. The Holy Roman emperor Charles IV made Prague his capital city and increased its size and importance by commissioning many new buildings.

JAN HUS

Above: A 15th-century illustration of Jan Hus being arrested for heresy. He was later put to death by burning—the normal punishment for heretics.

Jan Hus was born about 1372 in southern Bohemia and entered the University of Prague in about 1390. After graduating, he started to teach at the university at a time when the ideas of Wycliffe were percolating through the Czech student body. In 1402 Hus took charge of the Bethlehem Chapel, which had been founded for the express purpose of preaching in the Slavic language. Hus was influenced by many of Wycliffe's ideas, and most of his sermons were attacks on clerical corruption—a common, but not necessarily heretical, theme. Hus was excommunicated (banished from the church) by the archbishop of Prague in 1409. He remained in the Bohemian capital until 1412, when he was excommunicated again, this time by the pope, for preaching against indulgences (cancellations of punishment for sins). For the next two years he took refuge in the countryside. When the Council of Constance assembled in 1414, Emperor Sigismund promised Hus safe conduct to the council to defend his views. Despite Sigismund's promise, Hus was arrested, convicted of heresy, and burned at the stake.

was avoided due to the policies of King Wenceslas. However, when he died in 1419, open rebellion broke out.

The followers of Hus (called Hussites) were condemned as heretics by the Catholics, and a crusade was called against them. Armies of the Holy Roman Empire invaded Bohemia several times, only to be turned back by the brilliant military tactics of Jan Zizka, who organized mobile units of farm wagons with cannons mounted on them. After Zizka's death the Hussites' resistance crumbled, mainly because of divisions among them.

The moderate Hussites (called Utraquists) reached a compromise with the church at the Council of Basel in 1431, which gave them some limited religious freedom. The radical Hussites (called Taborites) refused to accept this compromise. Utraquists joined forces with Catholics to crush the Taborites—only to discover too late that the Catholics regarded the Basel compromise as temporary. Nevertheless, a version of the compromise remained in force until the early 17th century.

HAPSBURG RULE

Following the death of King Louis II at the battle of Mohács in 1526, the throne of Bohemia fell to the Hapsburgs when the largely Catholic nobility elected Archduke Ferdinand of Austria. The first century of Hapsburg rule was marked by economic decline. The mining industry suffered as gold and silver from the New World flooded the market. Bohemian resources were also drained by wars against the Ottoman Turks, who had conquered much of neighboring Hungary and were threatening Bohemia itself.

SEE ALSO
♦ Holy Roman Empire
♦ Reformation

Bologna

Bologna was not only one of the wealthiest cities of Renaissance Italy, it was also one of the most influential. Its wealth was based on the textile industry, and its influence was due to its university, a major center for the study of law.

During the 15th century Bologna had a population of about 50,000, but by the late 16th century that grew to 70,000. The city was part of the Papal States, but control swung between the church and several powerful families until Pope Julius II finally threw out the Bentivoglio family and restored the power of the papacy in 1506.

The city's great wealth came primarily from its involvement in the textile industry. Bolognese merchants sold hemp and wool, and the excellent silk produced by the region was in great demand. Other sources of revenue were agriculture and the university.

THE UNIVERSITY OF BOLOGNA

Bologna's university was one of the first established in Europe. From the 11th century it was an important center for the study of law. Bolognese scholars rediscovered Roman law, the study of which continued throughout the 12th century. During the Renaissance the growth of commerce and the increase in governmental bureaucracy created a high demand for men trained in law, and Bologna became an important center of learning and the largest Italian university.

In the 15th century, under the Bentivoglio family's patronage, art also flourished in Bologna, and artists continued to find work in the city in the 16th century, when the civic government commissioned various public works. The most important Bolognese artists were the Carracci family. Brothers Agostino (1557–1602) and Annibale (1560–1609), along with their cousin Ludovico (1555–1619), rejected the artificiality associated with the mannerist style of painting and pursued naturalism in art. Through the efforts of Ludovico the first formal art academy was set up in Bologna in the late 16th century.

Bologna also encouraged women artists. One famous example was Properzia de' Rossi (1490–1530), who gained prominence as a sculptor. Another was Lavinia Fontana (1552–1614), who painted mythological and biblical works and portraits.

Above: The center of the city of Bologna as it looks today. The large building in the background is the San Petronio Basilica. Work on this cathedral began in the late 14th century and continued throughout the Renaissance period.

SEE ALSO

♦ Baroque
♦ Italy
♦ Papal States
♦ Universities

Timeline

♦ **1305** Giotto begins work on frescoes for the Arena Chapel, Padua—he is often considered the father of Renaissance art.

♦ **1321** Dante publishes the *Divine Comedy*, which has a great influence on later writers.

♦ **1327** Petrarch begins writing the sonnets known as the *Canzoniere*.

♦ **1337** The start of the Hundred Years' War between England and France.

♦ **1353** Boccaccio writes the *Decameron*, an influential collection of 100 short stories.

♦ **1368** The Ming dynasty comes to power in China.

♦ **1377** Pope Gregory XI moves the papacy back to Rome from Avignon, where it has been based since 1309.

♦ **1378** The Great Schism begins: two popes, Urban VI and Clement VII, both lay claim to the papacy.

♦ **1378** English theologian John Wycliffe criticizes the practices of the Roman Catholic church.

♦ **1380** Ivan I of Muscovy defeats the army of the Mongol Golden Horde at the battle of Kulikovo.

♦ **1389** The Ottomans defeat the Serbs at the battle of Kosovo, beginning a new phase of Ottoman expansion.

♦ **1397** Sigismund of Hungary is defeated by the Ottoman Turks at the battle of Nicopolis.

♦ **1397** Queen Margaret of Denmark unites Denmark, Sweden, and Norway under the Union of Kalmar.

♦ **1398** The Mongol leader Tamerlane invades India.

♦ **1399** Henry Bolingbroke becomes Henry IV of England.

♦ **1400** English writer Geoffrey Chaucer dies, leaving his *Canterbury Tales* unfinished.

♦ **1403** In Italy the sculptor Ghiberti wins a competition to design a new set of bronze doors for Florence Cathedral.

♦ **c.1402** The Bohemian preacher Jan Hus begins to attack the corruption of the church.

♦ **1405** The Chinese admiral Cheng Ho commands the first of seven expeditions to the Indian Ocean and East Africa.

♦ **1415** Jan Hus is summoned to the Council of Constance and condemned to death.

♦ **1415** Henry V leads the English to victory against the French at the battle of Agincourt.

♦ **c.1415** Florentine sculptor Donatello produces his sculpture *Saint George*.

♦ **1416** Venice defeats the Ottoman fleet at the battle of Gallipoli, but does not check the Ottoman advance.

♦ **1417** The Council of Constance elects Martin V pope, ending the Great Schism.

♦ **1418** Brunelleschi designs the dome of Florence Cathedral.

♦ **1420** Pope Martin V returns the papacy to Rome, bringing peace and order to the city.

♦ **c.1420** Prince Henry of Portugal founds a school of navigation at Sagres, beginning a great age of Portuguese exploration.

♦ **1422** Charles VI of France dies, leaving his throne to the English king Henry VI. Charles VI's son also claims the throne.

♦ **c.1425** Florentine artist Masaccio paints the *Holy Trinity*, the first painting to use the new science of perspective.

♦ **1429** Joan of Arc leads the French to victory at Orléans; Charles VII is crowned king of France in Reims Cathedral.

♦ **1431** The English burn Joan of Arc at the stake for heresy.

♦ **1433** Sigismund of Luxembourg becomes Holy Roman emperor.

♦ **1434** Cosimo de Medici comes to power in Florence.

♦ **1434** The Flemish artist Jan van Eyck paints the *Arnolfini Marriage* using the newly developed medium of oil paint.

♦ **1439** The Council of Florence proclaims the reunion of the Western and Orthodox churches.

♦ **c.1440** Donatello completes his statue of David—the first life-size bronze sculpture since antiquity.

♦ **1443** Federigo da Montefeltro becomes ruler of Urbino.

♦ **1447** The Milanese people declare their city a republic.

♦ **1450** The condottiere Francesco Sforza seizes control of Milan.

♦ **1450** Fra Angelico paints *The Annunciation* for the monastery of San Marco in Florence.

♦ **1453** Constantinople, capital of the Byzantine Empire, falls to the Ottomans and becomes the capital of the Muslim Empire.

♦ **1453** The French defeat the English at the battle of Castillon, ending the Hundred Years' War.

♦ **1454–1456** Venice, Milan, Florence, Naples, and the papacy form the Italian League to maintain peace in Italy.

♦ **1455** The start of the Wars of the Roses between the Houses of York and Lancaster in England.

♦ **c.1455** The German Johannes Gutenberg develops the first printing press using movable type.

♦ **1456** The Florentine painter Uccello begins work on the *Battle of San Romano*.

♦ **1461** The House of York wins the Wars of the Roses; Edward IV becomes king of England.

♦ **1461** Sonni Ali becomes king of the Songhai Empire in Africa.

♦ **1462** Marsilio Ficino founds the Platonic Academy of Florence— the birthplace of Renaissance Neoplatonism.

♦ **1463** War breaks out between Venice and the Ottoman Empire.

♦ **1465** The Italian painter Mantegna begins work on the Camera degli Sposi in Mantua.

♦ **1467** Civil war breaks out in Japan, lasting for over a century.

♦ **1469** Lorenzo the Magnificent, grandson of Cosimo de Medici, comes to power in Florence.

♦ **1469** The marriage of Isabella I of Castile and Ferdinand V of Aragon unites the two kingdoms.

♦ **1470** The Florentine sculptor Verrocchio completes his *David*.

♦ **1476** William Caxton establishes the first English printing press at Westminster, near London.

♦ **1477** Pope Sixtus IV begins building the Sistine Chapel.

♦ **c.1477** Florentine painter Sandro Botticelli paints the *Primavera*, one of the first large-scale mythological paintings of the Renaissance.

♦ **1478** The Spanish Inquisition is founded in Spain.

♦ **1480** The Ottoman fleet destroys the port of Otranto in south Italy.

♦ **1485** Henry Tudor becomes Henry VII of England—the start of the Tudor dynasty.

♦ **1486** *The Witches' Hammer* is published, a handbook on how to hunt down witches.

♦ **1488** Portuguese navigator Bartholomeu Dias reaches the Cape of Good Hope.

♦ **1491** Missionaries convert King Nzina Nkowu of the Congo to Christianity.

♦ **1492** The Spanish monarchs conquer Granada, the last Moorish territory in Spain.

♦ **1492** Christopher Columbus lands in the Bahamas, claiming the territory for Spain.

♦ **1492** Henry VII of England renounces all English claims to the French throne.

♦ **1493** The Hapsburg Maximilian becomes Holy Roman emperor.

♦ **1494** Charles VIII of France invades Italy, beginning four decades of Italian wars.

♦ **1494** In Italy Savonarola comes to power in Florence.

♦ **1494** The Treaty of Tordesillas divides the non-Christian world between Spain and Portugal.

♦ **1495** Leonardo da Vinci begins work on *The Last Supper* .

♦ **1495** Spain forms a Holy League with the Holy Roman emperor and expels the French from Naples.

♦ **1498** Portuguese navigator Vasco da Gama reaches Calicut, India.

♦ **1498** German artist Dürer creates the *Apocalypse* woodcuts.

♦ **1500** Portuguese navigator Pedro Cabral discovers Brazil.

♦ **c.1500–1510** Dutch painter Hieronymus Bosch paints *The Garden of Earthly Delights*.

♦ **c.1502** Italian architect Donato Bramante designs the Tempietto Church in Rome.

♦ **1503** Leonardo da Vinci begins painting the *Mona Lisa*.

♦ **1504** Michelangelo finishes his statue of David, widely seen as a symbol of Florence.

♦ **c.1505** Venetian artist Giorgione paints *The Tempest*.

♦ **1506** The Italian architect Donato Bramante begins work on rebuilding Saint Peter's, Rome.

♦ **1508** Michelangelo begins work on the ceiling of the Sistine Chapel in the Vatican.

♦ **1509** Henry VIII ascends the throne of England.

♦ **1509** The League of Cambrai defeats Venice at the battle of Agnadello.

♦ **1510–1511** Raphael paints *The School of Athens* in the Vatican.

♦ **1511** The French are defeated at the battle of Ravenna in Italy and are forced to retreat over the Alps.

♦ **1513** Giovanni de Medici becomes Pope Leo X.

♦ **1515** Thomas Wolsey becomes lord chancellor of England.

♦ **1515** Francis I becomes king of France. He invades Italy and captures Milan.

♦ **c.1515** German artist Grünewald paints the *Isenheim Altarpiece.*

♦ **1516** Charles, grandson of the emperor Maximilian I, inherits the Spanish throne as Charles I.

♦ **1516** Thomas More publishes his political satire *Utopia.*

♦ **1516** Dutch humanist Erasmus publishes a more accurate version of the Greek New Testament.

♦ **1517** Martin Luther pins his 95 theses on the door of the castle church in Wittenburg.

♦ **1519** Charles I of Spain becomes Holy Roman emperor Charles V.

♦ **1519–1521** Hernán Cortés conquers Mexico for Spain.

♦ **1520** Henry VIII of England and Francis I of France meet at the Field of the Cloth of Gold to sign a treaty of friendship.

♦ **1520** Portuguese navigator Ferdinand Magellan discovers a route to the Indies around the tip of South America.

♦ **1520** Süleyman the Magnificent becomes ruler of the Ottoman Empire, which now dominates the eastern Mediterranean.

♦ **1520–1523** Titian paints *Bacchus and Ariadne* for Alfonso d'Este.

♦ **1521** Pope Leo X excommuicates Martin Luther.

♦ **1521** The emperor Charles V attacks France, beginning a long period of European war.

♦ **1522** Ferdinand Magellan's ship the *Victoria* is the first to sail around the world.

♦ **1523–1525** Huldrych Zwingli sets up a Protestant church at Zurich in Switzerland.

♦ **1525** In Germany the Peasants' Revolt is crushed, and its leader, Thomas Münzer, is executed.

♦ **1525** The emperor Charles V defeats the French at the battle of Pavia and takes Francis I prisoner.

♦ **1525** William Tyndale translates the New Testament into English.

♦ **1526** The Ottoman Süleyman the Magnificent defeats Hungary at the battle of Mohács.

♦ **1526** Muslim Mongol leader Babur invades northern India and establishes the Mogul Empire.

♦ **c.1526** The Italian artist Correggio paints the *Assumption of the Virgin* in Parma Cathedral.

♦ **1527** Charles V's armies overrun Italy and sack Rome.

♦ **1527–1530** Gustavus I founds a Lutheran state church in Sweden.

♦ **1528** Italian poet and humanist Baldassare Castiglione publishes *The Courtier.*

♦ **1529** The Ottoman Süleyman the Magnificent lays siege to Vienna, but eventually retreats.

♦ **1530** The Catholic church issues the "Confutation," attacking Luther and Protestantism.

♦ **1531** The Protestant princes of Germany form the Schmalkaldic League.

♦ **1531–1532** Francisco Pizarro conquers Peru for Spain.

♦ **1532** Machiavelli's *The Prince* is published after his death.

♦ **1533** Henry VIII of England rejects the authority of the pope and marries Anne Boleyn.

♦ **1533** Anabaptists take over the city of Münster in Germany.

♦ **1533** Christian III of Denmark founds the Lutheran church of Denmark.

♦ **1534** Paul III becomes pope and encourages the growth of new religious orders such as the Jesuits.

♦ **1534** Luther publishes his German translation of the Bible.

♦ **1534** The Act of Supremacy declares Henry VIII supreme head of the Church of England.

♦ **c.1535** Parmigianino paints the mannerist masterpiece *Madonna of the Long Neck.*

♦ **1535–1536** The Swiss city of Geneva becomes Protestant and expels the Catholic clergy.

♦ **1536** Calvin publishes *Institutes of the Christian Religion*, which sets out his idea of predestination.

♦ **1536** Pope Paul III sets up a reform commission to examine the state of the Catholic church.

♦ **1537** Hans Holbein is appointed court painter to Henry VIII of England.

♦ **1539** Italian painter Bronzino begins working for Cosimo de Medici the Younger in Florence.

♦ **1539** Ignatius de Loyola founds the Society of Jesus (the Jesuits).

♦ **1541** John Calvin sets up a model Christian city in Geneva.

♦ **1543** Andreas Vesalius publishes *On the Structure of the Human Body*, a handbook of anatomy based on dissections.

♦ **1543** Polish astronomer Copernicus's *On the Revolutions of the Heavenly Spheres* proposes a sun-centered universe.

♦ **1544** Charles V and Francis I of France sign the Truce of Crespy.

♦ **1545** Pope Paul III organizes the Council of Trent to counter the threat of Protestantism.

♦ **1545** Spanish explorers find huge deposits of silver in the Andes Mountains of Peru.

♦ **1547** Charles V defeats the Protestant Schmalkaldic League at the Battle of Mühlberg.

♦ **1547** Ivan IV "the Terrible" declares himself czar of Russia.

♦ **1548** Titian paints the equestrian portrait *Charles V after the Battle of Mühlberg.*

♦ **1548** Tintoretto paints *Saint Mark Rescuing the Slave.*

♦ **1550** Italian Georgio Vasari publishes his *Lives of the Artists.*

♦ **1553** Mary I of England restores the Catholic church.

♦ **1554** Work begins on the Cathedral of Saint Basil in Red Square, Moscow.

♦ **1555** At the Peace of Augsburg Charles V allows the German princes to determine their subjects' religion.

♦ **1556** Ivan IV defeats the last Mongol khanates. Muscovy now dominates the Volga region.

♦ **1556** Philip II becomes king of Spain.

♦ **1559** Elizabeth I of England restores the Protestant church.

♦ **1562** The Wars of Religion break out in France.

♦ **1565** Flemish artist Pieter Bruegel the Elder paints *Hunters in the Snow.*

♦ **1565** Italian architect Palladio designs the Villa Rotunda, near Vicenza.

♦ **1566** The Dutch revolt against the Spanish over the loss of political and religious freedoms:

Philip II of Spain sends 10,000 troops under the duke of Alba to suppress the revolt.

♦ **1569** Flemish cartographer Mercator produces a world map using a new projection.

♦ **1571** Philip II of Spain and an allied European force defeat the Ottomans at the battle of Lepanto.

♦ **1572** In Paris, France, a Catholic mob murders thousands of Huguenots in the Saint Bartholomew's Day Massacre.

♦ **1572** Danish astronomer Tycho Brahe sees a new star.

♦ **1573** Venetian artist Veronese paints the *Feast of the House of Levi.*

♦ **1579** The seven northern provinces of the Netherlands form the Union of Utrecht.

♦ **1580** Giambologna creates his mannerist masterpiece *Flying Mercury.*

♦ **1585** Henry III of France bans Protestantism in France; civil war breaks out again in the War of the Three Henrys.

♦ **1586** El Greco, a Greek artist active in Spain, paints the *Burial of Count Orgaz.*

♦ **1587** Mary, Queen of Scots, is executed by Elizabeth I of England.

♦ **c.1587** Nicholas Hilliard paints the miniature *Young Man among Roses.*

♦ **1588** Philip II of Spain launches his great Armada against England —but the fleet is destroyed.

♦ **1589** Henry of Navarre becomes king of France as Henry IV.

♦ **1592–1594** Tintoretto paints *The Last Supper.*

♦ **1596** Edmund Spencer publishes the *Faerie Queene*, glorifying Elizabeth I as "Gloriana."

♦ **1598** Henry IV of France grants Huguenots and Catholics equal political rights.

♦ **1598** In England the Globe Theater is built on London's south bank; it stages many of Shakespeare's plays.

♦ **1600–1601** Caravaggio paints *The Crucifixion of Saint Peter*, an early masterpiece of baroque art.

♦ **1603** Elizabeth I of England dies and is succeeded by James I, son of Mary, Queen of Scots.

♦ **1610** Galileo's *The Starry Messenger* supports the sun-centered model of the universe.

♦ **1620** The Italian painter Artemisia Gentileschi paints *Judith and Holofernes.*

Glossary

A.D. The letters A.D. stand for the Latin Anno Domini, which means "in the year of our Lord." Dates with these letters written after them are measured forward from the year Christ was born.

Altarpiece A painting or sculpture placed behind an altar in a church.

Amphitheater A large circular or oval building, often open to the sky, with tiers of seats ranged around a central space. It was used in ancient Rome for public spectacles such as games or gladiatorial contests.

Apprentice Someone (usually a young person) legally bound to a craftsman for a number of years in order to learn a craft.

Baptistery Part of a church, or a separate building, where people are baptized.

B.C. Short for "Before Christ." Dates with these letters after them are measured backward from the year of Christ's birth.

Bill of exchange A contract between a banker and his client in which the client borrows a sum of money in one currency and promises to repay it on a set date in another currency.

Bureaucracy A system of government that relies on a body of officials and usually involves much paperwork and many regulations.

Cameo A precious stone carved with a design that stands out from the background, often using the stone's different colors to enhance the effect.

Cardinal An official of the Catholic church, highest in rank below the pope. The cardinals elect the pope.

Classical A term used to describe the civilizations of ancient Greece and Rome, and any later art and architecture based on ancient Greek and Roman examples.

Colonnade A row of columns supporting an arched or a flat structure.

Condottiere A mercenary soldier, that is, a soldier who will fight for any employer in return for money.

Double-entry bookkeeping. A system of keeping accounts in which each transaction is entered twice, once as a credit entry to one account, and once as a debit entry to another.

Excommunicate To ban someone from taking part in the rites of the church.

Façade An architectural term for the front of a building, particularly one that is decorated.

Factor A merchant's agent operating in another country.

Flemish A word used to describe someone or something from Flanders, a region including present-day Belgium and parts of the Netherlands and France.

Fresco A type of painting that is usually used for decorating walls and ceilings in which pigments (colors) are painted into wet plaster.

Genre A term used to describe paintings depicting scenes from daily life.

Heresy A belief that is contrary to the accepted teachings of the church.

Heretic Someone whose beliefs contradict the teachings of the church.

Humanism A new way of thinking about human life that characterized the Renaissance. It was based on the study of "humanities"—that is, ancient Greek and Roman texts, history, and philosophy—and stressed the importance of developing rounded, cultured people.

Indulgences Cancelations of punishment for sins. Indulgences were often granted by the church in return for money.

Mason A builder, particularly one skilled in working in stone.

Orders A term used in classical architecture for the five different types of classical columns and the rules governing their use.

Ottava rima (eighth rhyme) A verse of eight lines that rhymes abababcc. It is of Italian origin, and Boccaccio helped establish it as the main form for Italian narrative verse.

Pastoral narrative A story set in the countryside that celebrates the attractions of a simple, rural existence.

Patron Someone who orders and pays for a work of art.

Patronage The act of commissioning and paying for a work of art.

Pediment A term used in classical architecture to describe the triangular-shaped structure at the top of a building façade (front); the term is also used for moldings above windows and doorways.

Pilaster An architectural feature consisting of a vertical strip that sticks out slightly from a wall like a flattened column.

Portico A term used in classical architecture to describe a roofed structure with columns and a pediment (see above) on the front of a building; also known as a temple front.

Prose The ordinary form of written language—that is, not poetry.

Sarcophagus A stone coffin, often decorated with carved panels.

Siege A military blockade of a castle or town to force it to surrender, often by cutting off its supplies of food and water.

Treatise A book or long essay about the principles, or rules, of a particular subject.

Triumphal arch A huge, freestanding arch decorated with sculpture built by the ancient Romans to celebrate a great military victory or leader. Processions passed through the arch as part of victory celebrations.

Vatican The headquarters of the pope and papal government in Rome.

Vernacular The language of the ordinary people of a country, rather than a literary or formal language like Latin.

Further Reading

Avery, Charles. *Bernini: Genius of the Baroque.* Boston, MA: Bulfinch Press, 1997.

Bardi, Piero. *The Atlas of the Classical World: Ancient Greece and Ancient Rome.* New York: Peter Bedrick Books, 1997.

Barter, James. *The Palace of Versailles.* San Diego, CA: Lucent Books, 1999.

Bartz, Gabriele. *Fra Angelico.* Cologne, Germany: Könemann, 1998.

Bazin, Germain. *Baroque and Rococo.* London: Thames & Hudson, 1985.

Bellonci, Maria. *Lucrezia Borgia.* London: Phoenix Press, 2000.

Bessire, Mark. *Great Zimbabwe.* Danbury, CT: Franklin Watts, 1999.

Boone, Elizabeth Hill. *The Aztec World.* Washington, DC: Smithsonian Books, 1994.

Brook, Larry. *Daily Life in Ancient and Modern Timbuktu.* Minneapolis, MN: Runestone Press, 1999.

Byam, Michèle. *Arms and Armor.* New York: DK Publishing, 2000.

Claridge, Amanda, Judith Toms, and Tony Cubberly. *Rome: An Oxford Archaeological Guide.* Oxford: Oxford University Press, 1998.

Cole, Alison. *Eyewitness: Renaissance.* New York: DK Publishing, 2000.

Conrad, David. *The Songhay Empire.* Danbury, CT: Franklin Watts, 1998.

Corrain, Lucia. *The Art of the Renaissance.* New York: Peter Bedrick Books, 1997.

Debus, Allen G. *Man and Nature in the Renaissance.* Cambridge, UK: Cambridge University Press, 1978.

Farber, Joseph C. and Henry Hope Reed. *Palladio's Architecture and Its Influence: A Photographic Guide.* New York: Dover Publications, 1980.

Ferino-Pagden, Sylvia, and Maria Kusche. *Sofonisba Anguissola: A Renaissance Woman.* Washington, DC: National Museum of Women in the Arts, 1995.

Fisher, Leonard Everett. *Galileo.* New York: Macmillan, 1992.

Gade, John A. *Life and Times of Tycho Brahe.* New York: Greenwood Press, 1969.

Garin, Eugenio. *Astrology in the Renaissance: The Zodiac of Life.* London: Routledge & Kegan Paul, 1983.

Grafton, Anthony. *Leon Battista Alberti: Master Builder of the Italian Renaissance.* New York: Hill & Wang, 2000.

Greenberg, Lorna, and Margot F. Horwitz. *Digging into the Past: Pioneers of Archeology.* Danbury, CT: Franklin Watts, 2001.

Henry, John. *Moving Heaven and Earth: Copernicus and the Solar System.* Cambridge, UK: Icon Books, 2001.

Henry, John. *The Scientific Revolution and the Origins of Modern Science.* New York: St. Martin's Press, 1997.

Hibbert, Christopher. *The House of Medici: Its Rise and Fall.* New York: Quill, 1980.

Hodge, Susie. *Ancient Roman Art.* Des Plaines, IL: Heineman Interactive Library, 1998.

Hood, William. *Fra Angelico: San Marco, Florence.* New York: George Braziller, 1995.

Howarth, Sarah. *Renaissance People.* Brookfield, CT: Millbrook Press, 1992.

Howarth, Sarah. *Renaissance Places.* Brookfield, CT: Millbrook Press, 1992.

January, Brendan. *Science in the Renaissance.* Danbury, CT: Franklin Watts, 1999.

Kelly, J.N.D. *The Oxford Dictionary of Popes.* Oxford: Oxford University Press, 1989.

Kerr, Daisy. *Knights and Armor.* Danbury, CT: Franklin Watts, 1997.

Koslow, Philip J. *Hausalan: The Fortress Kingdoms.* Broomall, PA: Chelsea House Publishing, 1995.

Koslow, Philip J. *Benin: Lords of the River.* Broomall, PA: Chelsea House Publishing, 1996.

MacDonald, Fiona. *Leonardo da Vinci.* Broomall, PA: Chelsea House Publishing, 2000.

Malpass, Michael A. *Daily Life in the Inca Empire.* Westport, CT: Greenwood Publishing, 1996.

Martell, Hazel Mary. *The Age of Discovery.* New York: Facts on File, 1993.

McLanathan, Richard. *Peter Paul Rubens.* New York: Harry N. Abrams, 1995.

Morley, Jacqueline. *A Renaissance Town.* New York: Peter Bedrick Books, 1996.

Morrison, Taylor. *Neptune Fountain: The Apprenticeship of a Renaissance Sculptor.* New York: Holiday House, 1997.

Murray, John Joseph. *Antwerp in the Age of Plantin and Brueghel.* Norman, OK: University of Oklahoma Press, 1970.

Perlingieri, Ilya Sandra. *Sofonisba Anguissola: First Great Woman Artist of the Renaissance.* New York: Rizzoli, 1992.

Romei, Francesca. *Leonardo da Vinci.* New York: Peter Bedrick Books, 1994.

Strieder, Jacob. *Jacob Fugger the Rich: Merchant and Banker of Augsburg, 1459–1525.* Westport, CT: Greenwood Press, 1984.

Summerson, John Newenham. *Inigo Jones.* New Haven, CT: Yale University Press, 2000.

Tarshis, Jerome. *Andreas Vesalius: Father of Modern Anatomy.* New York: Dial Press, 1969.

Tempestini, Anchise. *Giovanni Bellini.* New York: Abbeville Press, 1999.

White, Michael. *Galileo Galilei: Inventor, Astronomer, and Rebel.* Woodbridge, CT: Blackbirch Press, 1999.

Wilson-Smith, Timothy. *Caravaggio.* London: Phaidon Press, 1998.

WEBSITES

World history site
www.historyworld.net

BBC Online: History
www.bbc.co.uk/history

The Webmuseum's tour of the Renaissance
www.oir.ucf.edu/wm/paint/glo/renaissance/

Virtual time travel tour of the Renaissance
library.thinkquest.org/3588/Renaissance/

The Renaissance
www.learner.org/exhibits/renaissance

National Gallery of Art—tour of 16th-century Italian paintings
www.nga.gov/collection/gallery/ita16.htm

Uffizi Art Gallery, Florence
musa.uffizi.firenze.it/welcomeE.html

Database of Renaissance artists
www.artcyclopedia.com/index.html

Set Index

MAPS
The maps in this book show the locations of cities, states, and empires of the Renaissance period. However, for the sake of clarity, present-day place names are often used.